P9-ASB-820

WITHDRAWN

How to BUILD a
COIN
COLLECTION

How to
BUILD
a
Coin Collection

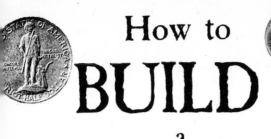

BY FRED REINFELD

Sterling Publishing Co., Inc. New York

Distributed to the coin trade by
President Coin Corporation

OTHER BOOKS OF INTEREST

Cash for Your Coins

Cash for Your Stamps

Catalogue of the World's Coins

Coin Collecting

Coin Collectors' Handbook

Coin Dictionary and Guide

Coinometry

Getting Started in Coin Collecting

Getting Started in Stamp Collecting

Hidden Values in Coins

Pictorial Guide to Coin Conditions

Picture Book of Ancient Coins

Story of Paper Money

Treasury of the World's Coins

U.S. Commemorative Coins and Stamps

ACKNOWLEDGMENTS

The author's thanks are due to David A. Boehm, publisher, for his tireless encouragement and close cooperation; to Burton Hobson for his knowledgeable suggestions and assistance; and to Sawyer McA. Mosser and the American Numismatic Society for supplying the remarkable condition pictures.

The Publishers acknowledge with thanks the work done for this edition by Beatrice Reinfeld.

CONTENTS

I. THE FASCINATION OF COIN COLLECTING

Collecting — collecting almost anything — is one of man's most enjoyable and satisfying hobbies. Some collecting hobbies are not easy to account for; for example, the specialist in bird calls, frog croaks, or locomotive whistles eagerly seizes on every record in his field. The attractions of coin collecting, on the other hand, immediately impress even those who have not yet become "numismatists."

Coins are beautiful

The most obvious appeal is that coins are beautiful — they are miniature works of art designed by outstanding artists. Most coins are pictorial and highly decorative, with simple or intricate designs — remarkable portraits, ships, maps, bridges, palaces and churches, railroads, flags and other patriotic images. It is easy to understand that one of the deepest pleasures of coin collecting comes from merely examining the items of a collection, one by one, and savoring the loving artistry that has gone into their painstaking production.

Coins contain history

Linked with art is the intense historical interest that surrounds coins as souvenirs of the past. In some cases this past is so remote that we would need to go to a museum to find any other remnant of it. Coins are perhaps the only reminders of past civilizations that we can acquire at little trouble and expense. That is why there is a special thrill in possessing coins of ancient Greece and Rome.

Such coins can widen our intellectual horizons and lead us into other fascinating hobbies. The collector who prizes his coin of Alexander the Great or the Emperor Nero will be led sooner or later to explore the eras in which these men lived; he will want to know more about the background of his coins.

As he pursues his quest he will see how historical traditions can live on for thousands of years. To take one outstanding example: the Greek figure of the goddess Athene was copied by the Romans in some of the female divinities pictured on their coins. This same figure in turn appeared as Brittania on English coins many centuries later!

Once we become aware of this historical appeal of coins, there is literally no limit to the fascinating byways through which this absorbing hobby will lead us.

Words on coins

The hold that tradition exerts is best exemplified in our debt to the Romans. As coin collectors, we soon discover that many of our most common numismatic terms stem from Latin. These include:

Coin, numismatics, obverse, reverse, inscription, design, commemorative coin, uncirculated coin, proof coin. All these are derived from Latin.

This is equally true of cent, dime, and quarter. And of course in our American motto seen on so many coins — *E pluribus unum* (or, "Many joined into one,") we have borrowed directly from the Latin.

(Left) United States, Jefferson type nickel, *reverse:* Jefferson's home at Monticello. Note motto on top: *E pluribus unum.*
(Right) Macedon, 336-323 B.C., gold double stater, *obverse:* head of Athene.

8

Mercury Head dime *obverse* (enlarged). Despite the popular name for this coin, the coin actually represents Liberty; the wings crowning the cap are intended to represent freedom of thought. This headdress can be traced back to many coins of ancient Greece and Rome.

Even the designs on the coinage of many countries — British, French, Spanish, and American, for example — have been directly borrowed from Roman originals. The Mercury dime which first appeared in 1916 is perhaps the clearest example of this. Here we have a head with a winged helmet — a design inspired by a Roman figure which was used for centuries on the denarius, a silver coin of about the same size as our dime. Even the very name of this coin, "dime," comes from an ancient English term — *"disme"* — which in turn goes back to old French; and even that origin can be traced further back to the Latin *decimus* — meaning "tenth." As a matter of fact, when the American dime was first issued in the 1790's, the name of the coin was spelled "disme."

Designs on coins

The use of stars and wreaths on many American coins goes back to Roman coins. So does our goddess of liberty, who is a "descendant" of the Roman goddesses, Roma and Libertas. Moreover, the diadem wreath worn by the American goddess — and her hair-do! — were inspired by Roman originals. The Liberty Cap often seen on the goddess also harks back to a Roman motif — the cap worn by freed slaves to show their new status.

One of the most Roman of American coins is the Peace

The Peace Dollar is one of the most Roman of all American coins. The radiate headdress was a favorite device on Roman imperial coinage.

Dollar, issued in the 1920's. This pictures the goddess of peace with rays around her head, a design borrowed from the radiate headdress used on portraits of Roman emperors to symbolize their "immortality." The Romans had copied this idea from the Persian sun-gods after sun-worship was imported into Rome from Persia.

To return for a moment to the Mercury dime: the reverse of this coin is full of Roman symbolism — the fasces (bundles of rods with an ax), which was the Lictor's badge of authority (later Mussolini's symbol); and the laurel wreath which was worn by triumphant Roman generals.

No motif has been more popular on American coins than the image of the eagle. This, too, was a favorite Roman religious symbol. The eagle was associated with Jupiter, which is why the standards of the Roman legions were topped with an eagle. The capture of such a standard by the enemy was considered a catastrophe, and its recapture even decades later was a cause for rejoicing. Napoleon copied this idea for his armies, but it is on American

The eagle is one of the favorite motifs on American coinage. The one pictured here appears on the reverse of the Liberty Seated Quarter.

The fasces (bundle of sticks with an ax) pictured here on the reverse of the Mercury Head Dime was a Roman symbol for power. The laurel wreath was the Roman reward for victory.

coins that the modern use of the eagle became most widespread. The eagle on American coins generally holds a cluster of arrows in its claws or a scroll in its beak. This too was a Roman device.

Identifying mintings

Finally, it is interesting to observe that another Roman device — the mint mark — is the chief index to the investment value of a coin. The mint mark is a small letter placed on the coin to indicate where it was struck, and the Romans first did this.

This brings us to a facet of coin collecting which is achieving ever greater prominence — collecting coins for profit. As the value of many coins goes up year after year, the collector of valuable coins can realize a handsome profit by eventually selling a coin after its price has increased considerably. In many cases the differential between the face value of a coin and its market value is considerable. In recent years the dividing line between coin collecting as a hobby and coin collecting as a form of investment has become hazier and hazier. As a numismatist becomes more experienced and more discriminating, pleasure and profit become increasingly intermingled.

But even the collector who is not in a position to follow up the investment angle or has no interest in it, can still find coins an absorbing hobby. In terms of sheer pleasure, he will spend many happy hours gathering, studying and arranging his collection, reading about the historical background of his coins, and making lasting friendships with other people who are equally interested in coin collecting.

Rome, 117-138 A.D., bronze sesterce, *reverse:* eagle. The popularity of this design on American coins can be traced back to the coins of ancient Greece and Rome.

2. HOW TO DETERMINE COIN VALUES

We have an instinctive reaction to the appearance of a coin, regardless of what its value may be. If it is bright and shiny and looks as if it has just come from the mint, we are instinctively pleased with its fresh appearance and its clear outline of design and lettering.

By the same token, a worn, faded coin repels us. It has had its day and we find it hard to be interested.

Coin conditions

These emotional reactions play a big part in determining coin values. Condition is a much more important factor in coin valuations than the beginner is apt to realize. A coin is a coin, he may think, and one specimen of it is as good as another.

Nothing could be farther from the truth. A coin selling for 25 cents in "fair" condition, for example, may sell for a hundred times that price in flawless condition. So we can conclude that collectors set enormous store by condition. In acquiring coins we must try to obtain them in the best possible condition we can afford. From the investment point of view, bear in mind that a coin in splendid condition, if it has other desirable features, tends to rise substantially in value over the years; whereas the same coin in poor condition will have a price that will rise sluggishly if at all. Hence it is foolish economy to buy coins in inferior condition. According to the same logic, your aim in trading should be to "trade up," always with the goal of improving the condition of your coins.

But, though condition is important, descriptions won't help us much if we use vague terms like "splendid" or "inferior." We need objective terms of reference on which all collectors can be agreed. The following definitions by Stuart Mosher, former editor of the *Numismatist,* are quoted from my book, *Coin Collectors' Handbook* (Sterling):

Proof (Pr.): a coin with a mirror-like surface struck with polished dies on a polished blank. Usually sold at a premium by the mints. (See page 117.)

Uncirculated (Unc.): in perfect condition, showing no signs of wear or damage but not necessarily brilliant.

Extremely Fine (Ex.F.): No definite signs of wear but having a less desirable surface than an uncirculated coin.

Very Fine (V.F.): showing inconsequential signs of wear but only slightly less desirable than the preceding classification.

Fine (F.): perceptible signs of wear but still a desirable piece.

Very Good (V.G.): definite signs of wear but not altogether unattractive.

Good (G.): worn but lettering and design all clear.

Fair (Fr.): quite badly worn and usually highly undesirable.

Poor (P.): less desirable than "fair" yet the design can usually be distinguished.

Armed with these descriptions, you can judge your own coins and have a clear understanding of descriptions in coin advertising matter. Bear in mind that an American coin with illegible date is worth no more than face value: the year of issue is a key factor in determining the premium value of an American coin.

UNCIRCULATED: All lettering and date extremely clear (note especially "LIBERTY" on headband). Diamond strokes on feathers and ribbon are all distinct. Ribbon appears clear and sharp. Hair above ribbon shows up strongly.

(Above) INDIAN HEAD CENT *obverse* (enlarged).
UNCIRCULATED
(Below) INDIAN HEAD CENT *obverse* (enlarged).
EXTREMELY FINE

EXTREMELY FINE: Very similar to uncirculated except that the highest points of the design, especially the hair around the ear and the ribbon where it crosses the beads, show the slightest signs of wear or rubbing. All fine detail is still clear and coins in this condition may have a little mint luster left.

15

VERY FINE: Design still quite clear. However, the coin begins to show definite signs of wear. The letters in "LIBERTY" are worn but the individual outline of each individual letter is still discernible. Only a partial outline of the diamonds on the ribbon appear, the middle two or three beads on the neck are worn smooth, and the tips of the feathers show smooth spots of wear.

(Above) INDIAN HEAD CENT *obverse* (enlarged).
VERY FINE
(Below) INDIAN HEAD CENT *obverse* (enlarged).
FINE

FINE: A considerably worn coin. The basic outline is still clear but most of the fine detail is lost. Only portions of the letters in "LIBERTY" still show. The diamond design on the ribbon is completely gone, only the end beads on the neck show, and all but the heaviest lines in the feathers are gone.

VERY GOOD: A much worn coin but free of serious gouges or other mutilation. The outlines of the head, letters and date are clear. "LIBERTY" is completely worn off, beads on neck no longer show, and there is no detail visible in feathers.

(Above) INDIAN HEAD CENT *obverse* (enlarged).
VERY GOOD
(Below) INDIAN HEAD CENT *reverse* (enlarged).
UNCIRCULATED

UNCIRCULATED: All details of wreath quite sharp. Horizontal and vertical bars on shield clearly outlined. Arrowheads and feathers distinct. Ribbon shows no signs of wear.

EXTREMELY FINE: Slight wear or rubbing on highest points, particularly the fine horizontal lines in shield and at the point where the ribbon is wrapped around the arrows.

(Above) INDIAN HEAD CENT *reverse* (enlarged).
EXTREMELY FINE
(Below) INDIAN HEAD CENT *reverse* (enlarged).
VERY FINE

VERY FINE: Wreath rather worn. Vertical bars on shield still distinct, but horizontal bars no longer sharp. Feathers on arrows less clear. Ribbon slightly worn.

FINE: Wreath definitely worn. Vertical bars in wreath are losing definition, horizontal bars distinctly faded. Feathers on arrows no longer show detail. Ribbon quite worn.

(Above) INDIAN HEAD CENT *reverse* (enlarged). FINE
(Below) INDIAN HEAD CENT *reverse* (enlarged). VERY GOOD

VERY GOOD: Vertical bars in shield still clear, but all other features considerably worn down and much detail lost.

Comparison of all these Indian Head obverses shows up the variations in condition. Lower right hand coin is in Good condition. Actual size.

Comparison of all these Indian Head reverses likewise
shows up the variations in condition.

UNCIRCULATED: Cheek and jawbones clearly defined. Lines of ear quite distinct. Bow-tie lines sharply outlined. Date is very clear. Hair in strong relief.

(Above) LINCOLN HEAD CENT *obverse* (enlarged).
UNCIRCULATED
(Below) LINCOLN HEAD CENT *obverse* (enlarged).
EXTREMELY FINE

EXTREMELY FINE: Slight wear or rubbing on the highest points of the design. The finest detail in the hair is worn and cheek, jawbone and bow-tie a little smooth.

VERY FINE: Hair around ear shows smooth spots and outline of ear is less distinct. Cheek and jawbone show definite smooth spots of wear.

(Above) LINCOLN HEAD CENT *obverse* (enlarged).
VERY FINE
(Below) LINCOLN HEAD CENT *obverse* (enlarged).
FINE

FINE: Jawbones clear but cheek somewhat faded. Most of detail gone on ear. Bow-tie lines less distinct. Date and mint mark still well defined. All detail of hair is gone.

VERY GOOD: Chin somewhat worn and all detail lost on cheek. Ear quite worn. Bowtie lines not too distinct. Date slightly worn.

(Above) LINCOLN HEAD CENT *obverse* (enlarged).
VERY GOOD
(Below) LINCOLN HEAD CENT *reverse* (enlarged).
UNCIRCULATED

UNCIRCULATED: Ears of grain and parallel lines are all sharp and distinct.

EXTREMELY FINE: Ears of grain and parallel lines still distinct. Inside row of wheat kernels are first point to show wear.

(Above) LINCOLN HEAD CENT *reverse* (enlarged).
EXTREMELY FINE
(Below) LINCOLN HEAD CENT *reverse* (enlarged).
VERY FINE

VERY FINE: Parallel lines are slightly smooth and the grains of wheat toward the top of branch are less distinct.

FINE: Parallel lines somewhat run together. Individual grains of wheat are visible but not very clearly defined.

(Above) LINCOLN HEAD CENTS *reverse* (enlarged).
FINE
(Below) LINCOLN HEAD CENTS *reverse* (enlarged).
VERY GOOD

VERY GOOD: Ears of grain and parallel lines almost worn smooth.

Comparison of all these Lincoln Head obverses shows up the variations in condition. Lower right coin is in Good condition. Actual size.

Comparison of all these Lincoln Head reverses likewise
shows up the variations in condition.

1959 Cent, reverse

UNCIRCULATED: Date quite sharp. Hair and braid show full detail.

(Above) INDIAN HEAD (or BUFFALO) NICKEL *obverse* (enlarged). UNCIRCULATED
(Below) INDIAN HEAD NICKEL *obverse* (enlarged). EXTREMELY FINE

EXTREMELY FINE: Date clear. Hair and braid fairly distinct.

29

VERY FINE: Date still clear. Braid distinct, but hair somewhat worn.

(Above) INDIAN HEAD NICKEL *obverse* (enlarged).
VERY FINE
(Below) INDIAN HEAD NICKEL *obverse* (enlarged).
FINE

FINE: Date somewhat faded but still readable. Fair detail on hair and braid.

VERY GOOD: Coin shows much wear and detail gone. Cheek worn smooth. Date must, of course, be identifiable although portions of the date and lettering may not be clearly defined.

(Above) INDIAN HEAD NICKEL *obverse* (enlarged).
VERY GOOD
·(Below) INDIAN HEAD NICKEL *reverse* (enlarged).
UNCIRCULATED

UNCIRCULATED: Horn shows distinctly. Hair on shoulder is clearly outlined.

EXTREMELY FINE: Horn still quite distinct. Hair on shoulder somewhat less clear.

(Above) INDIAN HEAD NICKEL *reverse* (enlarged). EXTREMELY FINE
(Below) INDIAN HEAD NICKEL *reverse* (enlarged). VERY FINE

VERY FINE: Hair on shoulder has lost much detail. Top of horn no longer distinct and horn has lost much of its roundness.

FINE: Horn hardly distinguishable. Hair on shoulder rather worn.

(Above) INDIAN HEAD NICKEL *reverse* (enlarged).
FINE
(Below) INDIAN HEAD NICKEL *reverse* (enlarged).
VERY GOOD

VERY GOOD: Horn worn smooth, hair on shoulder almost so.

Comparison of all these Indian Head Nickel obverses
shows up the variations in condition. Lower left coin
is in Good condition. Actual size.

Comparison of all these Indian Head Nickel reverses likewise shows up the variations in condition.

UNCIRCULATED: Very sharp detail on wings, helmet, and on hair above the forehead and in front of ear.

(Above) MERCURY HEAD DIME *obverse* (enlarged).
UNCIRCULATED
(Below) MERCURY HEAD DIME *obverse* (enlarged).
EXTREMELY FINE

EXTREMELY FINE: Hair slightly worn; part of wings worn smooth. Helmet fairly distinct.

VERY FINE: Much of detail lost on hair. More of helmet worn smooth. Helmet details less distinct. Less detail on wings.

(Above) MERCURY HEAD DIME *obverse* (enlarged).
VERY FINE
(Below) MERCURY HEAD DIME *obverse* (enlarged).
FINE

FINE: Most of fine detail on cap, hair and wings is gone although outline of wings and part of cap are still visible.

VERY GOOD: Hair worn smooth, as well as most of wings. Helmet shows considerable wear. General fuzziness from wear.

(Above) MERCURY HEAD DIME *obverse* (enlarged).
VERY GOOD
(Below) MERCURY HEAD DIME *reverse* (enlarged).
UNCIRCULATED

UNCIRCULATED: Rods in bundle are all sharply outlined. Diagonal bands and central band show out very clearly.

EXTREMELY FINE: Rods in bundle have lost some definition. Diagonal bands worn smooth but central band still quite clear.

(Above) MERCURY HEAD DIME *reverse* (enlarged).
EXTREMELY FINE
(Below) MERCURY HEAD DIME *reverse* (enlarged).
VERY FINE

VERY FINE: Much of the detail gone from the rods. Diagonal bands and central band very faint.

FINE: Rods almost completely worn smooth. Diagonal bands and central band no longer visible.

(Above) MERCURY HEAD DIME *reverse* (enlarged).
FINE
(Below) MERCURY HEAD DIME *reverse* (enlarged).
VERY GOOD

VERY GOOD: Rods and bands completely worn smooth. Lettering on motto is faint but readable. Some fading on outer inscription. Wreath somewhat worn.

Comparison of all these Mercury Head obverses shows
up the variations in condition.   Actual size.

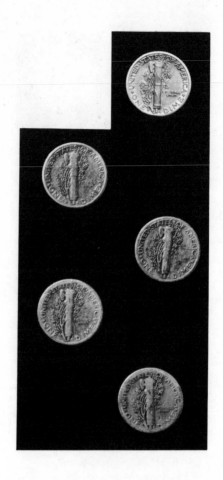

Comparison of all these Mercury Head reverses shows
up the variations in condition.

Liberty Head ("Barber") Quarter

Uncirculated

All the details are sharply outlined:

the shield	the eagle's claws
the eagle's eye	the arrows
the eagle's neck	the leaves
the eagle's feathers	the dots in the border

the dots between "United" and "Quarter" and between "America" and "Dollar"
the lettering on the inscription
the lettering on the ribbon

Liberty Head ("Barber") Quarter

Extremely Fine

All the details are still distinct.

Note, however, that there are slight scratches on the shield, and that the feathers are slightly faded toward the sides.

Very Fine

The eagle's eye and neck are distinct, and so are the arrows, the leaves, the dots and lettering on the inscription.

The shield is fairly distinct, but there are some nicks on it, and there are traces of fading toward the sides.

The feathers are considerably faded toward the sides, and the outside dots are beginning to grow fuzzy.

The claws are still fairly distinct, and so is the lettering on the ribbon, although *unum* is a little faded.

Fine

The shield and the eagle's eye are fairly distinct. However, there are some nicks and scratches on the shield and the fading toward the edges is getting more pronounced.

The neck is considerably faded, and the feathers are badly faded toward the sides.

The arrows, the leaves, and the lettering on the inscription are still distinct, and the dots in the inscription can be clearly seen.

The dots in the border have become fuzzier than in the previous condition.

The lettering on the ribbon is faded somewhat and several letters are unreadable.

The claws are no longer as distinct as they were previously (Note the "D" mint mark under the eagle.)

Very Good

The eagle's eye, the leaves, the dots and the lettering on the inscription are still distinct.

The lines on the shield are completely gone, and the details on the neck have almost disappeared.

Little of the detail on the feathers is left, and the claws seem to merge with the arrows and leaves.

The arrows have grown fuzzy, and the dots in the border are no longer distinct.

The lettering on the ribbon is badly faded and is becoming more unreadable.

	Proof		Uncirculated		Extremely Fin
Very Fine		Fine		Very Good	
	Good		Fair		Poor

Now look at these coins (in their exact size) side by side and notice the variation.

Liberty Head ("Barber") Quarters.

Foreign coin conditions

The foregoing discussion applies in the main to modern coins. When we come to older foreign coins, we have to apply somewhat different standards. American coinage dates only from the last decade of the eighteenth century, and Canadian coinage has had an even shorter life. Foreign coinage of course goes back much further.

Generally, the best condition of available coins issued before 1800 is "Fine." From 1800 to the early years of the twentieth century, we should be well satisfied with obtaining foreign coins in "Very Fine" condition. Coins in superior condition are occasionally found, and they command much higher valuations, depending on their condition. In more recent times, we may reasonably look for foreign coins in "Uncirculated" or "Extremely Fine" condition. During the past few years, some nations have issued "proof" sets of their coinage.*

Ancient coin conditions

Ancient coins, because of their considerable age, have to be judged by even more lenient standards. On the other hand, since they received comparatively little handling when in use, they may turn out to be in better condition than we might expect. These coins have to be judged on their individual features.

Each ancient coin, in other words, has to be judged on its interest for you. You may overlook the worn appearance of a Roman coin if it might have been handled by Julius Caesar or another luminary of the time.

Scarcity and demand

Aside from condition, the factor of supply *and* demand plays an important role in coin valuation. Mere rarity is not enough to determine a coin's value. A coin may be scarce, but if there is little or no demand for it, then it will not be valuable. Many foreign coins are rare, but their comparatively low prices are rising

*Note: Proofs are coins made especially for collectors at the mint. They are struck on polished planchets from polished dies which produce coins with brilliant mirror-like surfaces, sharp edges and perfect detail.

as more and more collectors turn to them because of the high price of many American coins.

In the case of American coins, the situation we find is quite different. The supply of already issued coins becomes smaller every year as coins disappear from circulation or into collections. The supply coming from break-up of collections cannot keep pace with the demand that comes from ever greater numbers of collectors of American coins.

The result is a steadily rising level in the value of American coins. Pent-up demand also influences collectors who intend at some time or other to sell some or all of their coins for profit-taking or emergency reasons. As the prices of American coins continue to go up, it is easy to dispose of such a collection at a good price, with no shortage of prospective buyers. Foreign coins present a somewhat different picture. Gold and other rare foreign coins always command a ready buyer. The prices of minor foreign coins and commoner pieces move more slowly than United States coins and therefore do not offer the same investment possibilities.

Mint marks

We have already seen that condition and demand play an important role in the valuation of coins. Tied in with the scarcity factor are mint marks. The United States has had seven mints, as follows:

Mint	Years	Mint Mark
Philadelphia, Pa.	1792 to date	none
Dahlonega, Ga.	1838-1861	D
Charlotte, N. C.	1838-1861	C
New Orleans, La.	1838-1909	O
San Francisco, Calif.	1854-1955	S
Carson City, Nev.	1870-1893	CC
Denver, Colo.	1906-1964	D

In only one case did the Philadelphia mint place mint marks on its coins: the silver content Jefferson Nickels from Philadelphia issued from 1942 to 1945 and a "P" mint mark. The new "sandwich" coins do not show mint marks regardless of where they are struck.

Mint marks have been an important guide to valuation of American coins as many coins have been issued in a single year by two or more mints.

If a coin dated 1964 or earlier has no mint mark, it was issued by Philadelphia. If it was issued by another mint, it has a letter showing where the coin was struck. Where there is a considerable difference in the quantities of a given coin struck in the same year at two or more mints, the coin issued in the smaller quantity will generally command a substantially higher price. Take the catalog valuation of the Lincoln head Cent (uncirculated) issued in 1925:

No mint mark (Philadelphia)	$ 9.00
"S" mint mark (San Francisco)	40.00
"D" mint mark (Denver)	30.00

To have this important information, we need to find the mint mark on the coin, as shown in the following pictures and table. We need also to know the quantities issued year by year of every coin. (These figures are given in *Coin Collectors' Handbook* and other coin catalogs, which also tell you when there was a multiple issue.) These figures are *generally* a good indication of the likely value of a coin, though there are cases where a coin is valuable despite the issue of a large number of coins. (For the mechanics and history of the minting process, see Chapter 6.)

Indian Head Cents: on the reverse, at the bottom under the wreath.

Lincoln Head Cents: on the obverse, under the date.

Three Cents — Silver: on the reverse, to the right of the "III."

Liberty Head Nickels: on the reverse, to the left of "cents."

Buffalo Nickels: on the reverse, under "Five cents."

Jefferson Nickels: on the reverse, to the right of the building, or above it.

Liberty Seated Half Dimes: on the reverse, under the wreath, or within it.

Liberty Seated Dimes: on the reverse, under the wreath, or within it.

Liberty Head Dimes: on the reverse, under the wreath.

Mercury Head Dimes: on the reverse, to the left of the fasces.

Roosevelt Dimes: on the reverse, at the left bottom of the torch.

Twenty Cent Pieces: on the reverse, under the eagle.

Liberty Seated Quarters: on the reverse, under the eagle.

Liberty Head Quarters: on the reverse, under the eagle.

Standing Liberty Quarters: on the obverse, above and to the left of the date.

Washington Quarters: on the reverse, under the eagle.

Liberty Seated Half Dollars: on the reverse, under the eagle.

Liberty Head Half Dollars: on the reverse, under the eagle.

Standing Liberty Half Dollars: on the reverse, to the left of "half dollar."

Franklin Half Dollars: on the reverse, above the Liberty Bell.

Kennedy Half Dollars: on the reverse, near the eagle's claw holding the laurel wreath.

Liberty Seated Dollars: on the reverse, under the eagle.

Liberty Head Dollars: on the reverse, under the eagle.

The mint mark on the Indian Head Cent (enlarged) appears on the reverse, at the bottom under the wreath.

Peace Dollars: on the reverse, at the bottom, to the left of the eagle's wing.

Trade Dollars: on the reverse, under the eagle.

Gold Dollars: on the reverse, under the wreath.

Ribbon Type Quarter Eagles: on the obverse, above the date.

Coronet Type Quarter Eagles: on the reverse, below the eagle.

Indian Head Type Quarter Eagles: on the reverse, to the left of the eagle's claw.

Three Dollar Gold Pieces: on the reverse, below the wreath.

Ribbon Type Half Eagles: on the obverse, above the date.

Coronet Type Half Eagles: on the reverse, below the eagle.

Indian Head Type Half Eagles: on the reverse, to the left of the eagle's claw.

Coronet Type Eagles: on the reverse, below the eagle.

Indian Head Type Eagles: on the reverse, to the left of the eagle's claw.

Coronet Type Double Eagles: on the reverse, below the eagle.

Liberty Standing Double Eagles: on the reverse, above the date.

(Above) The mint mark on the Liberty Head Nickel (enlarged) appears on the reverse, to the left of "cents." (Below) The mint mark on the Buffalo (or Indian Head) Nickel (enlarged) appears on the reverse, under "Five cents."

(Above) The mint mark on the Liberty Head Dime (enlarged) appears on the reverse, under the wreath. (Below) The mint mark on the Mercury Head Dime (enlarged) appears on the reverse, to the left of the fasces.

(Above) The mint mark on the Roosevelt Dime (enlarged) appears on the reverse, at the left bottom of the torch. (Below) The mint mark on the Standing Liberty Quarter (enlarged) appears on the obverse, above and to the left of the date.

(Above) The mint mark on the Washington Quarter (enlarged) appears on the reverse, under the eagle.

For mint mark on Barber type Quarter, *see* page 46.

What has been said here about the importance of mint marks should be kept in mind when reading Chapter 5. The more speculative aspects of buying and selling American coins depend in large part on mint marks, and this is even more emphatically true of price differentials in the case of rolls and proof sets (see pages 117 and 118).

The mint mark on the Liberty Head Half Dollar (enlarged) appears on the reverse, under the eagle.

The mint mark on the Standing Liberty Half Dollar (enlarged) appears on the reverse, to the left of "half dollar."

The mint mark on the Franklin Half Dollar (enlarged) appears on the reverse, above the Liberty Bell.

The mint mark on the Liberty Head Dollar (enlarged) appears on the reverse, under the eagle.

The mint mark on the Peace Dollar (enlarged) appears on the reverse, on the bottom, to the left of the eagle's wing.

3. WHAT KIND OF COLLECTION?

Topical collecting

The numismatist who has other hobbies can often combine them enjoyably with coin collecting. Thus, it is possible to build up a collection specializing in ship, railroad, building, or battle designs; or else to collect portraits of great men. There is an endless variety of beautiful coins along these lines.

National collecting

Most American collectors specialize in American coins. The chief reason is that most collectors of any nationality are likely to favor their own country's coins. *These are the coins they obtain most readily — in change —* so that they can build a very sizable collection with little difficulty or expense.

Then too, their own country's coins reflect history and traditions with which they are familiar and which appeal to their sense of patriotic pride.

Series and type collecting

Because American coins are so much in demand, they are collected by series or by types. In the case of *series collecting,* the objective is to build up a collection of a given series, trying to get one coin of each date and from each mint. This is the method applied to current or recently issued coins. In the case of the older coins, which by and large are substantially more expensive, *type collecting* is appropriate; this involves obtaining one coin of each design type. Any date or mint will do.

The beginning collector will do well to pick up all sorts of American coins in order to become familiar with them. Then he can decide which type or types he would like to specialize in. The two most modern varieties of cents are favorites because the coins are of the lowest denomination, are comparatively cheap, and, having been issued in large quantities, are still plentiful.

To get a general survey of the various types of U.S. coins, the following table will be useful.*

HALF CENTS (copper)

Liberty Cap	1793-1797
Draped Bust	1800-1808
Turban Head	1809-1836
Braided Hair	1840-1857

CENTS

Large Cents (copper)

Chain	1793
Wreath	1793
Liberty Cap	1793-1796
Draped Bust	1796-1807
Turban Head	1808-1814
Coronet	1816-1839
Braided Hair	1839-1857

Small Cents (copper-nickel 1856-1864; bronze 1864-1942, 1946 to date; steel 1943; copper 1944-1945)

Flying Eagle	1856-1858
Indian Head	1859-1909
Lincoln Head	1909 to date

TWO CENTS (bronze)

	1864-1873

* See chapter 7 for a list of catalog values.

Half Cent:
Liberty Cap Type

Half Cent:
Turban Head Type

Half Cent:
Draped Bust Type

Half Cent:
Braided Hair Type

LARGE CENTS

Cent: Chain, 1793,
reverse

Cent: Wreath, 1793.

Cent: Liberty Cap,
1794

Draped Bust, 1796

Turban Head, 1810

Left: Cent, Coronet Type (1817), obverse. *Right:* Cent, Braided Hair Type, (1839), so-called "booby head."

The Flying Eagle Cent, showing an eagle in graceful flight, is one of the handsomest American coins.

Two Cents Bronze

Three Cents Nickel

THREE CENTS—SILVER

FIVE CENTS—NICKEL

Shield Type   Liberty Head Type   Buffalo Type

Half Dime: Bust Type   Half Dime: Liberty Seated Type

 Left: Dime, Bust Type (1828). *Right:* Dime, Liberty Seated Type (1837).

Dime: Liberty Head Type

THREE CENTS (nickel)

	1865-1889

THREE CENTS (silver)

	1851-1873

FIVE CENTS (nickel)

Shield	1866-1883
Liberty Head	1883-1912
Buffalo	
(or Indian Head)	1913-1938
Jefferson	1938 to date

HALF DIMES (silver)

Bust (or Liberty Head)	1794-1837
Liberty Seated	1837-1873

Dime: Roosevelt Type

DIMES (silver)

Bust	1796-1837
Liberty Seated	1837-1891
Liberty Head	1892-1916
Winged Head Liberty ("Mercury Head")	1916-1945
Roosevelt	1946 to date

TWENTY-CENT PIECES (silver)   1875-1878

QUARTERS (silver)

Bust	1796-1838
Liberty Seated	1838-1891
Liberty Head (Barber)	1892-1916
Liberty Standing	1916-1930
Washington	1932 to date

Left: Quarter, Bust Type. *Right:* Quarter, Liberty Seated Type.

Below: Quarter, Liberty Head (Barber) Type (obverse)

Left: Quarter, Liberty Standing Type. *Right:* Quarter, Washington Type.

HALF DOLLARS (silver)

Bust	1794-1839
Liberty Seated	1839-1891
Liberty Head (Barber)	1892-1915
Liberty Standing	1916-1947
Franklin	1948 to date
Kennedy	1964-

Left: Half Dollar, Bust Type (1803). *Right:* Half Dollar, Liberty Seated Type (1840).

Liberty Head (Barber) Type Half Dollar

Half Dollar, Standing Liberty Type

Half Dollar, Franklin Type

Kennedy Type

69

Left: Dollar, Bust Type (1796). *Right:* Dollar, Liberty Seated Type (1840).

DOLLARS (silver)
Bust	1794-1839
Liberty Seated	1840-1873
Liberty Head (Morgan)	1878-1921
Peace	1921-1935

TRADE DOLLARS (silver)
	1873-1878
Proofs only	1879-1885

DOLLARS (gold)
Liberty Head	1849-1854
Indian Headdress	1854-1889

Dollar, Liberty Head (Morgan)
Type (obverse)

Dollar, Liberty Head (Morgan)
Type (reverse)

Trade Dollar (1873).
Left: obverse.
Right: reverse.

GOLD DOLLARS:

Liberty Head
Type

Indian-Head-
dress Type

Larger Indian-
Headdress
Type

QUARTER EAGLES:

Liberty Cap

Liberty Head

Ribbon Type

Coronet Type

Indian Head Incuse Type

THREE DOLLAR GOLD PIECE

QUARTER EAGLES ($2.50 gold)
             Liberty Cap   1796-1807
             Liberty Head   1808-1834
             Ribbon   1834-1839
             Coronet   1840-1907
             Indian Head Incuse   1908-1929

THREE DOLLAR GOLD PIECES   1854-1889

FOUR DOLLAR GOLD PIECES (Pattern Coins)
             Proofs only   1879-1880

FOUR DOLLAR GOLD PIECE

HALF EAGLES ($5 gold)
             Bust   1795-1834
             Ribbon   1834-1838
             Coronet   1839-1908
             Indian Head Incuse   1908-1929

EAGLES ($10 gold)
             Bust   1795-1804
             Coronet   1838-1907
             Indian Head   1907-1933

DOUBLE EAGLES ($20 gold)
             Coronet   1849-1907
             Liberty Standing
             (Saint-Gaudens)   1907-1933

HALF EAGLES:

Ribbon Type

Bust Type
Top: obverse.
Bottom: reverse.

Bust Type
Top: obverse.
Bottom: reverse.

Coronet Type
without motto

Indian Head Incuse Type

Eagle:

Bust Type

Coronet Type
with motto

EAGLE:

Coronet Type
without motto

Indian Head Type
without motto

Indian Head Type
with motto

Double Eagle, Coronet
Type without motto

Double Eagle, Saint-Gaudens Type

Collecting proof sets

During the years 1936-1942 and from 1950 to 1964, the Philadelphia mint issued the current cent, nickel, dime, quarter, and half dollar in a set made from special dies with exceptionally painstaking workmanship. When ordered in the year of issue from the mint, such a set cost $2.10 postpaid. Collectors hope that proof coinage will be resumed at some future date.

As you will see on pages 117 and 118, there has been a great deal of interest among collectors in purchasing such proof sets as a form of investment.

Commemoratives

Another type of American coinage which is of enormous interest to modern collectors is the whole field of commemorative coins.

As the name indicates, these coins were struck on special occasions, such as the Columbian Exposition (1893); the Pilgrim Tercentenary (1920); Oregon Trail Memorial (1926); Texas Centennial (1934). Aside from their historical interest, commemorative coins fascinate coin collectors because they are the most beautiful ever issued by the United States; in fact, among the most beautiful ever issued by any country.

Commemoratives were never intended to be used for general circulation. Hence, practically all of them are in uncirculated condition. So far there are 50 silver and 10 gold coins. The vast majority are silver half dollars.

Some of the commemorative coins continued to be issued for a number of years, and with several mint marks. The Booker T. Washington Memorial coin, for example, was issued for six years (1946-1951), in three varieties each year — no mint mark for the Philadelphia coin, "D" mint mark for the Denver coin, and "S" mint mark for the San Francisco coin. This makes 18 varieties in all, but only a keen specialist would be interested in having them all. By and large, however, collecting commemorative coins makes an attractive hobby where prices are not prohibitive.

COMPLETE LIST OF U. S. COMMEMORATIVES
SILVER COMMEMORATIVE COINS
(Half Dollars unless otherwise specified)

Year	Unc.	Year	Unc.
1892 Columbian Exposition	$5.00	1934 Daniel Boone Bicentennial	15.00
1893 Columbian Exposition	4.25	1935 Daniel Boone Bicentennial	12.50
1893 Isabella Quarter	95.00	1935 D Daniel Boone Bicentennial	17.50
1900 Lafayette Dollar	125.00	1935 S Daniel Boone Bicentennial	17.50
1915 S Panama-Pacific Exposition	85.00	1935 D-S (set of two)	35.00
1918 Illinois Centennial	25.00	1935 Daniel Boone Bicentennial	12.50
1920 Maine Centennial	25.00	1935 D Daniel Boone Bicentennial	200.00
1920 Pilgrim Tercentenary	12.50	1935 S Daniel Boone Bicentennial	200.00
1921 Pilgrim Tercentenary	17.50	1935 D-S (set of two)	400.00
1921 Missouri Centennial (with star)	175.00	1936 Daniel Boone Bicentennial	12.50
1921 Missouri Centennial (no star)	160.00	1936 D Daniel Boone Bicentennial	17.50
1921 Alabama Centennial (with 2 x 2)	90.00	1936 S Daniel Boone Bicentennial	17.50
1921 Alabama Centennial (no 2 x 2)	80.00	1936 D-S (set of two)	35.00
1922 Grant Memorial (with star)	200.00	1937 Daniel Boone Bicentennial	12.50
1922 Grant Memorial (no star)	25.00	1937 D Daniel Boone Bicentennial	175.00
1923 S Monroe Doctrine Centennial	17.50	1937 S Daniel Boone Bicentennial	175.00
1924 Huguenot-Walloon Tercentenary	27.50	1937 D-S (set of two)	350.00
1925 Lexington-Concord Sesquicent.	15.00	1938 Daniel Boone Bicentennial	
1925 Stone Mountain Memorial	7.50	1938 D Daniel Boone Bicentennial	
1925 S California Diamond Jubilee	30.00	1938 S Daniel Boone Bicentennial	
1925 Fort Vancouver Centennial	150.00	1938 P-D-S (set of three)	500.00
1926 Sesquicentennial of American		1935 Connecticut Tercentenary	60.00
Independence	17.50	1935 Arkansas Centennial	10.00
1926 Oregon Trail Memorial	15.00	1935 D Arkansas Centennial	15.00
1926 S Oregon Trail Memorial	15.00	1935 S Arkansas Centennial	15.00
1928 Oregon Trail Memorial	17.50	1936 Arkansas Centennial	
1933 D Oregon Trail Memorial	17.50	1936 D Arkansas Centennial	
1934 D Oregon Trail Memorial	15.00	1936 S Arkansas Centennial	
1936 Oregon Trail Memorial	12.50	1936 P-D-S (set of three)	35.00
1936 S Oregon Trail Memorial	17.50	1937 Arkansas Centennial	
1937 D Oregon Trail Memorial	12.50	1937 D Arkansas Centennial	
1938 Oregon Trail Memorial		1937 S Arkansas Centennial	
1938 D Oregon Trail Memorial		1937 P-D-S (set of three)	40.00
1938 S Oregon Trail Memorial		1938 Arkansas Centennial	
1938 P-D-S (set of three)	30.00	1938 D Arkansas Centennial	
1939 Oregon Trail Memorial		1938 S Arkansas Centennial	
1939 D Oregon Trail Memorial		1938 P-D-S (set of three)	100.00
1939 S Oregon Trail Memorial		1939 Arkansas Centennial	
1939 P-D-S (set of three)	150.00	1939 D Arkansas Centennial	
1927 Vermont Sesquicentennial	65.00	1939 S Arkansas Centennial	
1928 Hawaiian Sesquicentennial	500.00	1939 P-D-S (set of three)	450.00
1934 Maryland Tercentenary	35.00	1935 Hudson, N. Y. Sesquicentennial	250.00
1934 Texas Centennial	17.50	1935 S California-Pacific Exposition	22.00
1935 Texas Centennial		1936 D California-Pacific Exposition	30.00
1935 D Texas Centennial		1935 Old Spanish Trail	250.00
1935 S Texas Centennial		1936 Rhode Island Tercentenary	
1935 P-D-S (set of three)	45.00	1936 D Rhode Island Tercentenary	
1936 Texas Centennial		1936 S Rhode Island Tercentenary	
1936 D Texas Centennial		1936 P-D-S (set of three)	50.00
1936 S Texas Centennial		1936 Cleveland, Great Lakes Exposition	12.00
1936 P-D-S (set of three)	45.00	1936 Wisconsin Territorial Centennial	35.00
1937 Texas Centennial		1936 Cincinnati Musical Center	
1937 D Texas Centennial		1936 D Cincinnati Musical Center	
1937 S Texas Centennial		1936 S Cincinnati Musical Center	
1937 P-D-S (set of three)	50.00	1936 P-D-S (set of three)	275.00
1938 Texas Centennial		1936 Long Island Tercentenary	20.00
1938 D Texas Centennial		1936 York County, Maine Tercentenary	20.00
1938 S Texas Centennial		1936 Bridgeport, Conn. Centennial	40.00
1938 P-D-S (set of three)	100.00	1936 Lynchburg, Va. Sesquicentennial	50.00

)36 Elgin, Illinois Centennial.....................	50.00	
*36 Albany, N. Y. Charter.........	60.00	
*36 S San Francisco-Oakland Bay Bridge	30.00	
)36 Columbia, S. C. Sesquicentennial		
*36 D Columbia, S. C. Sesquicentennial		
*36 S Columbia, S. C. Sesquicentennial...		
1936 P-D-S (set of three).....................	125.00	
*36 Arkansas Centennial-Robinson..........	25.00	
*36 Delaware Tercentenary......................	50.00	
36 Battle of Gettysburg (1863-1938)......	50.00	
*36 Norfolk, Va. Bicentennial..................	75.00	
*37 Roanoke Island, N. C. (1587-1937)...	30.00	
37 Battle of Antietam (1862-1937).........	85.00	
38 New Rochelle, N. Y. (1688-1938).....	65.00	
*46 Iowa Centennial................................	20.00	
46 Booker T. Washington Memorial.....	2.00	
*46 D Booker T. Washington Memorial...	3.50	
46 S Booker T. Washington Memorial...	2.50	
1946 P-D-S (set of three)...................	7.50	
47 Booker T. Washington Memorial		
47 D Booker T. Washington Memorial		
47 S Booker T. Washington Memorial		
1947 P-D-S (set of three)....................	15.00	
48 Booker T. Washington Memorial		
48 D Booker T. Washington Memorial		
48 S Booker T. Washington Memorial		
1948 P-D-S (set of three)..................	25.00	

1949 Booker T. Washington	
1949 D Booker T. Washington	
1949 S Booker T. Washington	
1949 P-D-S (set of three)...	35.00
1950 Booker T. Washington	
1950 D Booker T. Washington	
1950 S Booker T. Washington	
1950 P-D-S (set of three) ..	40.00
1951 Booker T. Washington	
1951 D Booker T. Washington	
1951 S Booker T. Washington	
1951 P-D-S (set of three) ..	30.00
1951 Carver-Washington	
1951 D Carver-Washington	
1951 S Carver-Washington	
1951 P-D-S (set of three) ..	15.00
1952 Carver-Washington	
1952 D Carver-Washington	
1952 S Carver-Washington	
1952 P-D-S (set of three) ..	22.50
1953 Carver-Washington	
1953 D Carver-Washington	
1953 S Carver-Washington	
1953 P-D-S (set of three) ..	20.00
1954 Carver-Washington	
1954 D Carver-Washington	
1954 S Carver-Washington	
1954 P-D-S (set of three) ...	17.50

GOLD COMMEMORATIVE COINS

ar (*Dollars unless otherwise specified*) Unc.

)3 Louisiana Purchase (Jefferson)...............	100.00
)3 Louisiana Purchase (McKinley).............	100.00
)4 Lewis and Clark Exposition....................	450.00
)5 Lewis and Clark Exposition....................	425.00
*5 S Panama-Pacific Exposition...................	75.00
*5 S Panama-Pacific Exposition ($2.50)......	400.00
5 S Panama-Pacific Exposition	
($50 round)..	5,000.00
5 S Panama-Pacific Exposition	
($50 octagonal)..................................	4,500.00
6 McKinley Memorial.................................	100.00
7 McKinley Memorial.................................	150.00
2 Grant Memorial (with star).....................	350.00
2 Grant Memorial (no star)........................	400.00
6 Philadelphia Sesquicentennial ($2.50)....	75,00

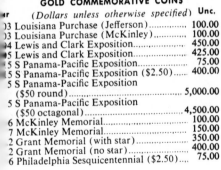

Above) Columbian Exposition Half Dollar. *Obverse:* Christopher Columbus. *Reverse:* Santa *Maria*. (Right) Lafayette Commemorative Dollar.

(Left) Isabella Commemorative Quarter issued for the Columbian Exposition of 1893. (Right) Panama-Pacific Exposition Commemorative Half Dollar, 1915.

(Above, left) Illinois Centennial, 1918, *obverse:* Abraham Lincoln. (Above, center) Maine Centennial, 1920, *obverse:* state coat of arms. (Above, right) Missouri Centennial, 1921, *reverse:* Indian and frontiersman.

(Above, left and center) Pilgrim Tercentenary, 1920, *obverse:* Governor William Bradford; *reverse: Mayflower.* (Above, right) Grant Memorial, 1922, *reverse:* birthplace of Gen. Grant.

(Above, left) Monroe Doctrine Centennial, 1923, *reverse:* map of the Western Hemisphere; (above, center) New Rochelle Commemorative, 1938, *reverse:* fleur-de-lis from city seal; (above, right) Stone Mountain Memorial, 1925, *obverse:* Genls. Robert E. Lee and Stonewall Jackson.

(Above, left and center) Lexington-Concord Sesquicentennial, 1925, *obverse:* Minute Man; *reverse:* Old Belfry at Lexington; (above, right) Fort Vancouver Centennial, 1925, *reverse:* Pioneer.

(Above, left) California Diamond Jubilee, 1925, *obverse:* Forty-niner; (above, center and right) Oregon Trail Memorial, 1926, *obverse:* Indian; *reverse:* covered wagon.

(Above, left) Vermont Sesquicentennial, 1927, *reverse:* catamount; (above, center) Hawaiian Sesquicentennial, 1928, *reverse:* native chief; (above, right) Texas Centennial, 1935, *obverse:* eagle on five-pointed star.

Above, left) Daniel Boone Bicentennial, 1935, *obverse:* Daniel Boone; (above, center) Connecticut Tercentenary, 1935, *obverse:* Charter Oak; (above, right) Arkansas Centennial, 1936, *reverse:* eagle guarding symbol of American flag.

Canadian coins

The foreign country whose coins have the greatest interest for Americans is Canada. There are obvious reasons. Sharing a common border and a common language, the two countries have many contacts with each other. Canada's coins are the ones which reach the United States most readily.

More specifically, American collectors are interested in Canadian coins because, as U.S. coins have come into short supply, more and more collectors are turning to Canadian coins as a suitable substitute. Canadian coinage goes back only a century or so and there have been quite a few changes in design. Consequently, it is less difficult than in the case of American coins to assemble a complete set of any given type. Another factor which favors the beginning collector is that mint marks are relatively infrequent in Canadian coinage; and as we have seen earlier, coins with mint marks are apt to be more expensive.

Canadian coins always picture the reigning British monarch on the obverse. The royal portraits are as follows:

Victoria	1858-1901
Edward VII	1902-1910
George V	1911-1936
George VI	1937-1952
Elizabeth II	1953 to date

The denominations which are now current are:

small cents	1920 to date
5 cents nickel	1922 to date
10 cents silver	1858 to date
25 cents silver	1870 to date
50 cents silver	1870 to date
silver dollars	1935 to date

Coin holders are available for these types, as well as for other coins which have been discontinued.

Up to 1935 Canadian coins were issued with reverses which carried numerical values in a wreath. But the dollar which was

Large Cent (Queen
Victoria on obverse).

Large Cent (Edward
VII on obverse).

Large Cent (George
V on obverse).

25 Cents Sil-
ver, George
VI on ob-
verse with
Caribou Head
reverse.

Queen Elizabeth II

10 Cents Sil-
ver, Fishing
Schooner re-
verse.

5 Cents Nickel
(George VI
on obverse,
with beaver
reverse).

Dollar: Voyageur Type

Dollar: Cabot Sailing
Ship Type

81

issued that year marked a new trend. Since then the Canadian reverses have all been pictorial and extremely attractive. There are five types of dollar reverses: *voyageurs* (canoemen); the Parliament buildings; John Cabot's sailing ship; the 1958 totem pole coin; and the 1964 symbolic flower.

Other reverses are equally picturesque —

1 cent reverse: maple leaf.
5 cents reverse: beaver.
10 cents reverse: fishing schooner.
25 cents reverse: caribou head.
50 cents reverse: arms of Canada.
1 dollar reverse: Voyageur and Indian in canoe.

Some of the five-cent coins are unusual in that they are twelve-sided instead of having the conventional round shape.

Elizabeth II (*obverse*), beaver (*reverse*)
on 12-sided 5-cent piece

A recent dollar — the 1958 British Columbia Commemorative — achieved a good deal of notoriety because it pictures a totem pole on the reverse. The Indians of British Columbia protested strenuously against this coin, as they believe by tradition it will bring bad luck.

Collectors of Canadian coins like to buy the mint sets which are issued every year. These attractive coins have an investment value and are increasing in popularity.

These "proof-like" coins are "select, uncirculated" specimens packaged by the Canadian mint at Ottawa. The coins used in these sets are in the best possible condition and therefore highly desirable for collections. The supply of sets is limited and usually disposed of early in the year.

British coins

Coins of foreign countries are collected by types, not by dates, as the interest in them is not great enough to warrant such specialization. English coins are of great historical interest, especially the "gun money" of James II (actually issued in Ireland) and the "Maundy" sets which are still being issued during the reign of Queen Elizabeth II. *

1902, Silver Maundy money, *reverses:* crown over value for fourpence, threepence, twopence, and penny.

1689, Brass shilling, *obverse:* James II; *reverse:* crown over crossed scepters. A coin made from melted-down cannon and issued by James II in Ireland during the revolt of 1689.

Other coins of historical interest are those issued in the eighteenth century and counterstamped "Vigo" or "Lima" to show that they were struck from bullion seized from Spanish galleys. Another picturesque coin, issued in 1800, shows the likeness of George III counterstamped on a Spanish Piece of Eight.

In the twentieth century, British designers turned to pictorial motifs for the reverses of the coins. These coins are unusually handsome and therefore very rewarding to collect. Proof sets are issued on occasions of national significance, such as the Festival of Britain in 1951 and the 1953 Coronation, and these are well worth having.

* The presentation of Maundy money has been one of the most interesting customs connected with the British monarchy. It is described in detail in *Treasury of the World's Coins* (Sterling).

1668, Silver crown, *obverse:* laureate bust of Charles II; *reverse:* crowned shields.

1800. This Spanish Dollar ("Piece of Eight") was issued by Spain in 1795 with the bust of Charles IV on the obverse. In 1800 Great Britain reissued the coin with a small countermarked bust of George III, and gave the coin an official valuation of 4 shillings, 9 pence.

1846, Silver crown, *obverse:* Victoria ("young head" type); *reverse:* crowned arms.

1849, Silver florin, *obverse:* Victoria; *reverse:* shields. (Known as the "Godless Florin" because the words *Dei Gratias* were omitted.)

1954, Bronze halfpenny, *reverse:* the *Golden Hind* (Sir Francis Drake's flagship).

1935, Silver crown, *reverse:* St. George and the Dragon. Issued for George V's silver jubilee.

(*Left*) 1953, copper-nickel crown, *obverse*: Elizabeth II on horseback (coronation commemorative). (*Right*) 1956, copper-nickel crown, *reverse*: portrait of Sir Winston Churchill.

85

(Above, left) South Africa, 1947, silver crown, *reverse:* springbok gazelle.
(Above, right) South Africa, 1952, silver crown, *reverse:* ship. This coin commemorates the tercentenary of the founding of Cape Town.

(Above, left) Southern Rhodesia, 1932, silver 2 shillings, *reverse:* antelope;
(above, center) Southern Rhodesia, 1932, silver shilling, *reverse:* stone bird;
(above, right) Rhodesia and Nyasaland, 1955, copper-nickel half crown,
reverse: arms.

(Left) Australia,
1937, silver crown,
reverse: crown.

(Above) New Zealand, 1949, silver
crown, *reverse:* leaf with stars (to commemorate
proposed royal visit); (left)
New Zealand, 1933, silver florin, *reverse:*
kiwi bird.

Likewise the coinage of other parts of the British Commonwealth — South Africa, Australia, New Zealand, Fiji, Cyprus, Ceylon, and Rhodesia, for example — includes many fine reverses. All coins of Great Britain, the dominions and the colonies carry the likeness of the reigning monarch on the obverse. The proof sets, like those of Canada and Great Britain, merit the attention of collectors as outstandingly beautiful coins.

European coins

Pictured here is a sample collection of European coins:

Among French coins, those of the French Revolution and Napoleonic period are of outstanding interest. But there are many fine portraits on later coins, particularly those of Napoleon III. Many modern French colonial coins have attractive designs.

(Above, left) France, 1791, brass 12 deniers, *obverse:* Louis XVI; *reverse:* fasces in wreath surmounted by Liberty Cap.

(Above) France, 1795, silver 1 sol, *obverse:* tablet reading: "All men are equal before the law"; *reverse:* Liberty Cap, wreath, and scales to denote justice.

(Above, left) France, 1812, silver 5 francs, *obverse:* Napoleon; *reverse:* wreath with value.

87

German coinage is a vast and extensive subject. The old talers of the German states, going back to the seventeenth century, include some of the finest coins ever struck. Many of the very early German coins are available for less than $10 each — about the price of a U.S. 1931S Cent. These issues have been neglected because many collectors are unaware of them.

In the nineteenth century the German states issued a variety of coins, many with finely executed designs, which are attractive to the average collector, and also provide an interesting field for later specialization.

The commemorative issues of the German Republic during the 1920's and 1930's are very colorful and varied. Few collectors will be able to resist their appeal.

(Above, left) Brunswick, 1634-66 silver 1¼ taler, *obverse:* four fields with Neptune on a dolphin, heron baiting, mine, alchemy; *reverse:* Fortuna on globe, sailing ship in background.

(Left) Germany, 1927, silver 3 marks, *obverse:* two figures (commemorates the thousandth anniversary of the founding of Nordhausen; (right) Germany, 1928, silver 3 marks, *obverse:* medieval sculpture (commemorates the thousandth anniversary of the founding of Dinkelsbuhl).

(Above, left) Saxony, 1610-15, silver taler, *obverse:* 4 Saxon dukes; (above, right) Saxe-Weimar, 1908, silver 5 marks, *obverse:* bust of Duke Johann Friedreich (commemorating 350th anniversary of the founding of the University of Jena).

(Right) Erfurt, 1631, silver "Purim" taler inspired by an Old Testament text, *obverse:* rays with Hebrew lettering; *reverse:* inscription commemorating the victory of Gustavus Adolphus at Breitenfeld.

eft) Germany, 1929, silver 3 marks, *obverse:* President Hindenburg; (center) *verse:* uplifted fingers pledging loyalty to the constitution; (right) Germany, 30, silver 3 marks, *obverse:* Zeppelin encircling world.

(Above, left) Eire, 1939, silver florin, *obverse:* harp; (above, right) *reverse:* salmon.

(Above, left) Israel, 1949, bronze 1... prutahs, *obverse:* amphora; (above right), *reverse:* value in wreath.

Eire, or Ireland, has issued very few coins, but they are likewise irresistible — and fortunately most reasonably priced. The same applies to the coins of Israel, although as issues become obsolete they become harder to obtain and consequently more desirable.

Austrian coinage falls roughly into three categories. The old talers of the period 1600-1800 have all the attractiveness of the ornate, finely executed designs which mostly picture the Holy Roman Emperors. Many of these coins are very moderately priced.

The subsequent coinage of the Hapsburgs has some interesting coins, including the famous Maria Theresa talers. These can be obtained at quite reasonable prices, and are among the "must" items of any representative collection.

The Austrian Republic, like its German counterpart, issued some beautiful coins which are by no means expensive. Of special interest are the commemoratives picturing Schubert, Mozart, Haydn and Beethoven.

Franz Schubert   Wolfgang Mozart   Josef Haydn

(Left) Counts Schlick of Joachimstal, 1525, silver taler, *obverse:* St. Joachim. This was the first taler ("dollar") coin, a type which became extremely popular all over Europe and in other parts of the world as well.

(Right) Fugger, 1694, silver taler, *obverse:* family coat of the Fuggers, for generations the richest and most powerful bankers of Europe.

(Left) Austria, 1780, silver taler, *obverse:* Maria Theresa; (right) *reverse:* coat of arms. This is the famous Maria Theresa Taler, issued by Austria for more than a century and a half, but always dated 1780. These coins were used extensively in trading with the Levant, the Middle East, and Africa.

(Left) Papal States, 1676-89, silver scudo, *obverse:* Pope Innocent XI; *reverse:* St. Peter's.

Italian coinage is one of the most varied in the world, due to the fact that for centuries Italy was split up into tiny states and cities. The Papal coins are perhaps outstanding in this field; the artistry of the designs and the significance of the religious symbols give these coins a unique distinction.

Both under the Italian monarchy (after 1870) and the subsequent Fascist regime, many interesting coins were struck in an effort to evoke some of the glories of ancient Rome. These coins bring home to us the tenacity with which historical traditions are sometimes retained for thousands of years. This classical spiri has been maintained in the coins issued by the Italian Republic

(Left) Italy, 1926-30, silver 10 lire, *obverse:* Victor Emmanuel; (center) *rever* biga (two-horse chariot); (right) Italy, 1946-51, aluminum 10 lire, *obver* Pegasus.

(Left) Greece, 1930, 20 drachmai, *obverse:* Poseidon; (right) *reverse:* prow of galley.

Twentieth-century Greek coins (including copies of ancient masterpieces) are moderately priced, as are many Italian coins. A number of other twentieth-century foreign coins are available for ten cents; a few minor ones cost more than $1.00.

(Left) Spanish milled dollar (Piece of Eight, so called because the denomination was 8 reales). It was sometimes divided into eight parts ("bits") to make change (center). This explains how the American quarter got its name, and why it is colloquially referred to as "two bits." (Right) Spain, 1889-92, silver 5 pesetas, *obverse:* baby head of Alfonso XIII.

The extensive Spanish coinage has one item that ought to appear in any representative collection — the Spanish 8 reales coin, or Piece of Eight, as it is more popularly known. Because of the glamorous tradition of Spanish galleons and pirate treasure, these coins have an irresistible appeal for many collectors.

(Left) Portugal, 1928, silver 10 escudos, *obverse:* mounted Knight; (center) *reverse:* Portuguese arms commemorating the Battle of Ourique, fought in 1139; (right) Belgium, 1935, silver 50 francs, *reverse:* exhibition hall. Issued for the railroad centenary.

Portuguese coinage includes the colorful commemorative issue of 1898 and attractive commemorative coins of the twentieth century with picturesque designs.

Belgium has issued some interesting commemorative coins and finely executed portrait coins, which have the advantage of being easily obtainable.

Modern Dutch coins are not particularly notable, but many of the old talers and other coins issued in the sixteenth and seventeenth centuries are very handsome.

(Left) Switzerland, 1922-26, 1931-54, silver 5 francs, *obverse:* William Tell; (center) Switzerland, 1934, silver 5 francs, *obverse:* Swiss guard; (right) *reverse:* crowned arms in wreath.

Switzerland has issued a large number of colorful coins, among them the coinage specially struck for shooting festivals. Sweden has likewise issued attractive modern commemoratives, and the old coins of the seventeenth and eighteenth centuries also include some remarkable designs.

(Above, left) Leyden, 1574, silver taler, *obverse:* Sennacherib's mighty Assyrian host melting away before Jerusalem—note the Biblical reference to 2 Kings: 19; (above, right) *reverse:* Spaniards fleeing from Leyden. One of the most remarkable commemorative coins ever issued.

(Above) Netherlands, 1941-43, zinc 10 cents, *obverse:* tulip (issued by the German occupation government). (Right) Luxembourg, 1946, silver 50 francs, *obverse:* King John the Blind mounted on horseback.

(Left) Danzig, 1932, aluminum-bronze, *obverse:* cod fish; (center) Estonia, 1934, aluminum-bronze kroon, *obverse:* Viking ship; (right) *reverse:* Estonian arms.

(Above, left) Iceland, 1930, silver 10 kronur, *obverse:* King of Thule with kneeling children; (above, right) *reverse:* shield with supporters. Issued to commemorate the 1000th anniversary of Iceland's parliament.

(Above, left) Denmark, 1659, silver crown, *obverse:* arm from heaven cutting off the (Swedish) hand which tries to seize crown; (above, right) Hungary 1506, silver ½ taler, *obverse:* St. Ladislaus on horseback.

(Left) Poland, 1936, silv 5 zlotych, *obverse:* saili ship; *reverse:* eagle.

(Above, left) Russia, 1913, silver rouble, *obverse:* Nicholas II and Michael Feodorovich; (above, right) *reverse:* crowned double eagle (tercentenary of the Romanov dynasty).

(Above) Latvia, 1929, 1931-32, silver 5 lati, *obverse:* peasant girl.

(Above) Hungary, 1938, silver 5 pengo, *obverse:* St. Stephen (900th anniversary of his death).

(Above, left) San Marino, 1931-37, silver 20 lire, *obverse:* crown over 3 feathers; (above, right) *reverse:* St. Marinus.

(Left) Sweden, 1921, silver 2 kronor, *obverse:* Gustavus Vasa; (right) *reverse:* arms (400th year of political liberty).

Albania, 1926-28, silver 2 franka ari, *obverse:* sower.

AFRICA

(Above, left) Somalia, 1950, bronze 10 centesimi, *obverse:* elephant; (above, right) *reverse:* star over value.

(Above) Cameroons, 1943, aluminum-bronze franc, *obverse:* rooster.

(Above, left) Belgian Congo, 1943, brass 2 francs, *obverse:* elephant; (above, right) *reverse:* value.

(Above) East Africa, 1936, copper 10 cents, center hole, *reverse:* elephant tusks.

ASIA

(Left) Lebanon, 1925-40, aluminum-bronze 5 piastres, *obverse:* cedar; (right) *reverse:* galley.

(Left) India, 1950-51, 1953-54, copper-nickel anna, scalloped edge, *obverse:* Asoka pillar; (right) *reverse:* Brahma bull.

Asian coins

Among coins of Asia, there are interesting items from India, China, Japan, Burma, Thailand, Indo-China. One bar to collecting these coins has been the unfamiliarity of the languages and the consequent difficulty of identifying coins.

(Above) Siam, 1868-1910, silver tical, *reverse:* three umbrellas.

(Above) China, 1932, silver dollar, *obverse:* Chinese junk, birds, sun, and value.

(Left) Burma, 1852-78, silver rupee, *obverse:* peacock; (right) Japan, 1953, bronze 10 yen, *reverse:* temple.

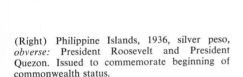

(Right) Philippine Islands, 1936, silver peso, *obverse:* President Roosevelt and President Quezon. Issued to commemorate beginning of commonwealth status.

Latin-American coins

Turning to the New World, the coins of outstanding interest are the colorful commemoratives of Mexico and Brazil. However, other countries, such as Cuba, Argentina, Uruguay, have issued handsome memorials of Bolivar, San Martin and other revolutionary heroes. The Central American countries have some interesting issues devoted to the age of the Conquistadors.*

(Above) Argentina, Rio de la Plata Provinces, 1836, silver 8 reales, *reverse:* sun-symbol.

(Above) Venezuela, 1879, 1886-89, 1900-37, silver 5 bolivares, *obverse:* Simon Bolivar.

Mexico, 1953, silver 5 pesos, *obverse:* Miguel Hidalgo (200th anniversary of his birth).

Mexico, 1947-48, silver 5 pesos, *obverse:* Cuauhtemoc.

---

* For current prices of coins illustrated here, see pages 151-153. For other foreign coins, with illustrations and prices, see *A Catalogue of the World's Most Popular Coins* (Sterling).

(Left) Spain, Guatemala mint, 1791-1806, silver 8 reales (Piece of Eight), *reverse:* Spanish arms. (Right) Guatemala, 1824-48, silver 8 reales, *obverse:* mountain range.

(Above) Panama, 1930, 32-34, silver ½ balboa, *obverse:* Vasco Nunez de Balboa.

(Above, left) Honduras, 1931-37, silver lempira, *obverse:* Indian chief Lempira; (above, right) *reverse:* Honduran arms.

(Left) Cuba, 1953, silver peso, *reverse:* rising sun; (center) Colombia, 1947-48, silver 50 centavos, *obverse:* Simon Bolivar; (right) Dominican Republic, 1937, bronze centavo, *obverse:* palm tree.

101

ANCIENT GREECE

(Above) Pergamum, about 190 B.C., silver stater, *reverse:* bowcase between two serpents.

(Above, left) Thrace, 323-281 B.C., silver tetradrachm, *obverse:* Alexander the Great; (above, right) *reverse:* Athene. The most famous coin of antiquity.

(Left) Egypt, about 310 B.C., silver tetradrachm, *obverse:* Alexander the Great with a headdress of an elephant scalp.

ANCIENT ROME

(Left) Rome, 54-68 A.D., bronze sesterce, *obverse:* Nero; (right) *reverse:* closed temple of Janus.

Rome, 134-138 A.D., bronze sesterce, *obverse:* Hadrian, one of the greatest of the emperors.

Ancient coins

Ancient coins — mainly those of Greece and Rome — do not receive the attention they deserve. No collection is really complete without the famous coins picturing Alexander the Great, one of the Athenian coins picturing the goddess Minerva and her owl, and some examples of Roman imperial coins. For sheer artistry these coins have never been excelled. Fortunately, while many ancient coins are in short supply, a good many are quite inexpensive. Nevertheless, this is a field which has been unjustly neglected.

While this survey of world coinage is concentrated only on the high spots, it does give the beginning collector an idea of the richness and variety and artistic achievement of world coinage. This is a field in which each individual collector will perhaps come on new discoveries that will delight him and intensify his interest in a lifetime hobby.

(Above) Rome, about 40 B.C., silver denarius, *reverse:* Roman temple of Juno Moneta (the guardian or "monitor"). This was the location of Rome's mint.

(Above, left) Rome, 103-111 A.D., bronze as, *obverse:* Trajan, another great emperor; (above, right) *reverse:* Trajan's bridge over the Danube.

(Left) Rome, 98-117 A.D., bronze sesterce, *reverse:* the Circus Maximus, which seated 260,-000 spectators; (right) Rome, 79-81 A.D., bronze sesterce, *reverse:* the Colosseum, another huge stadium.

103

4. HOW TO TAKE CARE OF COINS

To the novice, this may not seem to present any real problem. Coins, being made of metal, are obviously durable.

Actually, there are important precautions to take to prevent your coins from deteriorating. Naturally, you will want to keep them in the best possible condition; for, as we have seen, condition is an important key to coin values. Careless handling can also affect the condition of your coins. Many a beautiful and valuable coin has been ruined by a foolish attempt to clean it or shine it up.

Handling coins

How you handle your coins, then, will definitely affect the value of your collection. So keep these rules in mind:

1. Coins should be held by the edges. The novice who repeatedly lets his fingers come in contact with the surface of a coin runs the danger of causing the outline to fade because of the injurious effect of perspiration.

2. Coins kept unwrapped in a bag or box or purse are likely to develop scratches. Therefore, avoid placing coins in such containers.

3. Dropping or tapping coins to listen to their ring is another bad habit to avoid.

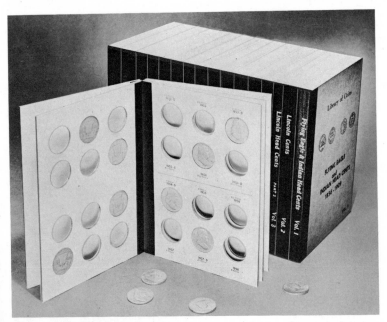

The best kind of coin album for storing United States coin types of various denominations. Such an album is highly convenient and provides excellent protection for the stored coins.

Coin albums

A collector who specializes in American coins — and this applies to the overwhelming majority of American collectors — has a great variety of useful equipment to choose from. If you are collecting series — Buffalo Nickels, say, or Lincoln Head Cents — you have three convenient ways of storing the coins that belong to any particular type. You can use (a) coin albums or (b) coin folders or (c) coin holders.

All three provide spaces which have been cut to size to fit all or most of the coins of a particular type. Often there are special spaces for all the different mint marks involved.

Each album page is made up of horizontal rows of openings in which coins are to be inserted. You slide out a section of transparent plastic, put in your coin or coins face up, then slide back the plastic to the "closed" position. The coin is now firmly in

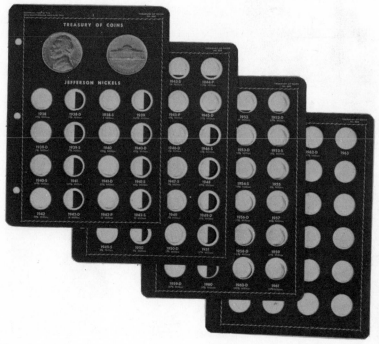

Looseleaf album pages allow the collector some flexibility in arranging his collection. They allow you to take out and display only the pages you want. Single pages can also be framed to make a wall display of coins.

place. You can see its obverse through the plastic and its reverse by turning the page. To take the coin out, you simply reverse the process.

You can obtain ring-binder albums with loose-leaf pages. For currently issued coin types, new sheets are continually being placed on the market to keep the album up to date. All the principal types of American coins are represented. In addition, there are special album pages for commemorative issues, proof sets, and some outstandingly popular foreign issues.

To support the weight of the coins, the album pages are made of double-thick cardboard. Generally the album pages have printed notations to show the placement of each coin. But plain albums and pages are also available, making it possible for the collector to make his own arrangements and descriptions of coins.

Coin folders

Cardboard coin folders are much cheaper and are made for more than forty different types of U.S. coins, as well as Canadian types. Here you get economy if you are willing to put up with a minor drawback: the coin reverses are not visible. To put the coin in its proper place, it is necessary to press it into a pre-cut opening. The coin rests against the cardboard back of the folder.

Coin holders of lucite are among the most attractive means of displaying your highly-prized coins.

Coin holders

The most attractive method of displaying coins is through the use of plastic holders. The best ones are made of lucite and are comparatively expensive. (The range of prices is approximately from $1.50 to $5.00 per holder.) They are usually made to hold a set or limited number of coins, and have a top and bottom plate. The coins are placed into the proper grooves on the bottom plate. The top plate is then fastened on with screws, and both obverses and reverses are visible.

Thus the coins appear to best advantage, and at the same time they are protected against tarnish. Quite a few of the beautiful proof sets of Great Britain, Canada, South Africa and Australia are available in special holders or cases.

107

Individual coin envelopes and holders

Individual cardboard holders are ideal for displaying collections of assorted coins. They are available with different sized openings. Coin envelopes provide space for a complete write-up about the coin.

You may prefer to put each of your coins in an individual cardboard holder or store them in 2″ x 2″ coin envelopes which provide more space for a write-up about each piece.

Coin envelopes are made of heavy paper in several colors, glassine, or cellophane. If you use either of the last two materials, you will be able to see the obverse and reverse of each coin without having to open the envelope and handle the coin. In any event, all three materials will protect your coins against dust, tarnish and moisture.

Using transparent envelopes will not only protect your coins; they will also enable you to classify the coins by means of an admirable filing system. This is how it works. You place the coin in a transparent envelope and fold over the top quarter-inch. Then you type all the necessary information about the coin — description, condition, date and amount of purchase, etc. — on a 2x2 area of an index card. After cutting out the 2x2 area, you staple it to the folded top of the envelope. Thus you have the related information right with the coin. A further refinement on this system is to use cards of different colors to indicate the various coin conditions. Now you are ready to set up your collection in systematic subdivisions — by type or country or topical subject. No matter how large your collection may become, these careful indexing methods will make it possible to pick out any given coin with a minimum of delay.

Storage boxes

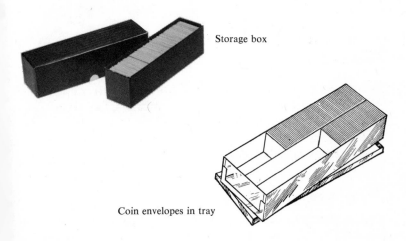

Storage box

Coin envelopes in tray

You can purchase storage boxes made of lightweight steel or heavy chipboard. The steel boxes measure about 2″ x 4″ x 14″ and hold a few hundred coins.

Inside, the box is fitted with adjustable dividers for storing 2x2 envelopes or holders. These are held firmly in place and cannot slip out. It is claimed that the box will hold a thousand coins.

Coin roll storage

The growing popularity of collecting American coins in rolls (page 118) for investment purposes has brought several handy

Coin rolls in containers: 50 pennies; 40 nickels; 50 dimes; 40 quarters; 20 half dollars.

products on the market. Coin tubes made of plastic are available for storing rolls of cents, nickels, dimes, quarters, half dollars, and silver dollars.

Rolls can also be stored in a steel storage box which accommodates coins of all denominations.

Cleaning coins

The problem of cleaning coins is one of the collector's perennial worries. Since the experts lay so much stress on fine condition, collectors are naturally troubled by signs of deterioration in a coin.

Thus, copper or bronze coins eventually take on a patina caused by the action of the oxygen in the air. This involves a change in the color of the coin — to green or black or brown or red or blue, or some combination of these colors, depending upon the amount of moisture in the atmosphere and the local composition of the soil. We always find this characteristic patina on ancient copper and bronze coins.

All silver coins tarnish in time, no matter how carefully you protect them. Even the most brilliant proof and uncirculated silver coins cannot be kept immune from this process. Consequently some collectors are led to use tarnish-removers and coin-cleaners

110

to restore their coins to their original condition. Such restoration work is always risky, and in many cases has resulted in new flaws.

Since the results of cleaning cannot be accurately foreseen, and since even the experts disagree on the advisability of cleaning, it is best to refrain.

Some collectors like to lacquer their silver coins. This will protect the coins against tarnish, to be sure, but the work must be done expertly.

Another caution to be kept in mind is that while you may like the lacquered appearance of your coins, others may not share your taste. Consequently, by lacquering your coins you may be unwittingly reducing the disposal value of your collection.

5. BUILDING UP YOUR COIN COLLECTION

It has been estimated that there are several million coin collectors in the United States. The annual amount of coin sales is thought to be in the neighborhood of $250,000,000 a year.

At least half the collectors in the United States are interested, primarily or exclusively, in American coins. To many of them, coin collecting is not only a delightful hobby — they view it, to some extent, as a means of investment.

Pocket change

How does a coin collector get started? In the case of American coins, he generally begins with pocket change. Inevitably he concentrates on the lower denominations currently being minted — Lincoln Head Cents, Jefferson Nickels, Roosevelt Dimes. Soon he is absorbed in meeting the challenge of completing the type set — getting a coin for every year and mint mark issued.

Soon our typical collector begins to branch out. His interest is attracted by lower-denomination coins which, though they are no longer being minted, have been discontinued so recently that they are still fairly common in pocket change. This applies to Buffalo Nickels (discontinued after 1938); Mercury Head Dimes (discontinued after 1945); and, to a lesser extent, Indian Head Cents (discontinued after 1909).

Up-grading

By now our beginner is acquiring some useful numismatic experience. Once he starts on the discontinued coins that are available in pocket change, he picks up two very important ideas. He soon realizes that he cannot get older coins in top condition but can get almost flawless specimens of the currently issued coins in the year of their apperance. This makes him condition-conscious, even if he has not yet realized the tremendous importance of condition in determining coin values. He keeps replacing poor specimens with more attractive ones, and this process of up-grading his collection becomes second nature.

Finding scarcer issues

He also finds that while it is reasonably possible to assemble a complete series of a currently issued coin, some dates are more common than others. He begins to wonder why this should be so, and this inquiring attitude is bound to lead him to the discovery that the quantities of coins issued vary from year to year.

His understanding of the situation is sharpened by his experiences with the discontinued coins that are available in circulation. The condition of these older coins is understandably inferior. Some dates seem hopelessly unobtainable. Thus he is led to the realization that if he wants to complete the series, he may have to buy some coins instead of relying on picking them up in pocket change.

Coin publications

Now his knowledge of numismatics begins to broaden in various ways. He may hear from friends about dealers who can supply the coins he wants. He learns that there are coin catalogs which list complete issues with market values for various conditions. And the enormous importance of mint marks will at last be brought home. Sooner or later he will establish a firm relationship with one or more dealers on whom he will rely for reasonable prices, satisfactory quality, dependable descriptions of coins, and for generally helpful and sound advice.

Trading with other collectors will help him to build up his collection or improve its quality. In this way he can rid himself of unwanted duplicates in return for coins that he lacks. However, his main reliance will continue to be on dealers, so it is important to know a few basic facts about coin trade practices.

Trade practices

Just what do we mean by the "value" of a coin? The value quoted in sale catalogs* is the approximate price you would have to pay if you wanted to *buy* a coin. It is by no means the price you would get for the same coin ("its premium value") if you were to sell it to the dealer. Obviously his buying price has to be substantially lower than his selling price for the same coin, if he is to stay in business, cover his expenses, and realize a suitable profit on his operations. (There are "premium" catalogs† on the market which list the prices dealers will pay.) Advantages of this method are immediate cash return and no necessity for such procedures as advertising and cataloguing.

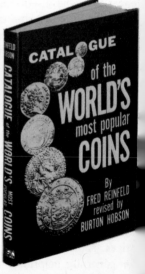

Catalogues such as *Coin Collectors' Handbook* (U.S. and Canadian) and *The Catalogue of the World's Most Popular Coins* show the prices dealers are currently charging for coins. Premium guides such as *Appraising and Selling Your Coins* show the prices dealers will pay for coins they can use in their stock.

---

* See chapter 7 for a list of catalog values.

Investing in coins

This brings us to the purchase of coins for investment. One theory of coin investment holds that coins should be purchased at their lowest price — as they are issued. (In the case of mint proof sets, a small fee must be paid to the mint, over and above the face value of the coins.) Then the coins should be held for a time (say ten years) in order to profit from the ensuing appreciation in the value of the coins.

While this method is good in theory, it must be applied in a flexible manner. Some coins will go up rapidly in value; others will move sluggishly. Some coins may even fluctuate in value from year to year, or they may level off temporarily. Thus, timing of buying and selling turns out to be of the utmost importance, and keen judgment of market trends is required. This leads logically to concentration on the "controller" coins, the scarce items in a series.

A collector finds it fairly easy and inexpensive to obtain the common coins of a type, but sooner or later he comes to want the coins of the series that are comparatively scarce. The only way is to pay high premiums for them. These coins, then, are known as the "controller" coins because they are the ones that the market-wise coin investor will be most interested in. Analysis of price trends shows that controller coins are not only much higher in price than those of the common coins of the series, but they also are the ones which show the most rapid increases.

Here is a useful list of the chief controller coins in the current series:

Lincoln Head Cents: 1909S (VDB); 1909S; 1910S; 1911S; 1912S; 1913S; 1914D; 1914S; 1915S; 1921S; 1922S; 1923S; 1924D; 1924S; 1926S; 1931D; 1931S; 1933D; 1960 small date.
Jefferson Nickels: 1938D; 1938S; 1939D; 1939S; 1942D; 1949S; 1950; 1950D; 1951S; 1955.
Roosevelt Dimes: 1949S; 1950S; 1951S; 1952S; 1955; 1955D; 1955S.

Washington Quarters: 1932D; 1932S; 1936D; 1940D; 1949; 1955D.

Franklin Half Dollars: 1948; 1949; 1953; 1955; 1956.

Other coins of these series which have promising investment possibilities are:

Lincoln Head Cents: 1932; 1933; 1939D; 1954; 1955S.

Jefferson Nickels: 1938D; 1938S; 1950D; 1951S.

Roosevelt Dimes: 1947S; 1954S; 1955P; 1955D; 1955S.

Among the older issues discontinued in the twentieth century, the most desirable coins by far are those in proof or uncirculated condition. The chief controller coins in these series are:

Indian Head Cents: 1864 (L on Ribbon); 1869; 1870; 1871; 1872; 1877; 1908S; 1909S. In general, the issues of the 1870's and 1880's are the scarcest in this series.

Buffalo Nickels: Almost all the D and S coins through 1928 have already risen so steeply as to be beyond the reach of the average collector, unless he is content with the inferior conditions.

Mercury Head Dimes: 1916D; 1919D; 1919S; 1921P; 1921D; 1926S; 1927D; 1942D (over '41). Among short issues which look promising are 1930S; 1931D; 1931S.

Standing Liberty Quarters: 1916; 1917D,S (two varieties); 1918S (over '17); 1919D,S; 1923S; 1926S; 1927S. Comparatively short issues which are still reasonably priced include 1926D; 1927D; 1929D,S; 1930S.

Standing Liberty Half Dollars: 1916; 1917D,S; 1919P,D,S; 1921P,D,S; 1938D. Most of these are so high in extremely fine or uncirculated condition as to price the ordinary collector out of the market. Among short issues which are still reasonably priced, 1916 is outstanding.

As for the series of commemorative coins, they have been issued in such small quantities that they have experienced considerable price rises in recent years. While there has been a certain amount of leveling off in the last few years, the trend is still upward.

Proof sets

There has been a sensational rise in the prices of proof sets. A proof set consists of the cent, nickel, dime, quarter, and half dollar (face value $.91). Through 1964, proof sets could be purchased from the Philadelphia mint for $2.10 issue price. Proof coinage has been temporarily suspended in order to free equipment to cope with the shortage of small change.

These specially selected coins have no imperfections. They are washed in a solution of cream of tartar and then rinsed in alcohol after having been stamped out much more slowly than coins intended for general circulation. The result of all this painstaking treatment is that all the details of the design stand out with unusual clarity.

As more and more collectors became interested in proofs, the number of sets issued annually by the government rose as well, reaching a record high of 3,752,919 in 1964.

Here is a comparison of the premium values on proof sets, taken from the 1956 and 1965 issues of *Coin Collectors' Handbook:*

Year	Initial Cost	1956	1965
1936	$1.81	$65.00	$750.00
1937	1.81	30.00	300.00
1938	1.81	20.00	150.00
1939	1.81	17.50	125.00
1940	1.81	15.00	100.00
1941	1.81	11.00	85.00
1942	1.81	12.00	85.00
1950	2.10	10.00	150.00
1951	2.10	6.00	75.00
1952	2.10	4.50	50.00
1953	2.10	3.00	35.00
1954	2.10		20.00
1955	2.10		25.00
1956	2.10		15.00

Roll coins

We can discern an equally notable trend in the investment purchase of rolls of coins in "brilliant uncirculated" condition. A roll of cents or dimes contains 50 coins; there are 40 coins in a roll of nickels or quarters; half dollars come in rolls of 20.

Purchase of coins in rolls considerably reduces their unit cost. Bought singly, they would cost much more.

Gold coins

There is considerable demand for gold coins, especially since a great many non-collectors hoard them — however, the initial cost is fairly high. Territorial gold coins (coins issued by California and other territories before they became states) comprise a highly specialized and expensive field and therefore hold no interest for the general run of collectors.

(During the nineteenth century, private individuals and organizations occasionally issued gold coins or stamped gold ingots. These issues, which resulted from a scarcity of regular United States coinage, had no connection with the United States mint. As most of these issues took place in the western states and territories, they are generally referred to as "territorial gold"; sometimes the term "private gold" is used.)

Timing

As was pointed out earlier, timing is all important in buying and selling. After constant price rises there are breathing spells when prices level off; then, later on, the upward trend is resumed. The collector who studies the movements of coin prices will be careful to buy when prices have temporarily leveled off, and avoid selling during those periods.

When prices are going up steadily, the problem is much more complicated. It takes very good judgment and plenty of experience on the collector's part to determine whether a price rise has reached its peak for the time being, or whether the upward movement is to continue. Thus, buying and selling decisions become extremely complex.

Any collector who contemplates investing in coins should realize before he starts that he will have to deal with a great many complex variables: the amounts he will have available for investment; the length of time he can sit back and wait for a substantial profit; the general trend of financial, economic and business conditions; the profit that might be realized from alternative investments; changes in fashion among coin collectors; the possibility that certain coins might be subject to speculative manipulation.

Considering all these problems, the small collector might come to the conclusion that he would do better to stick to numismatics as an enjoyable, absorbing hobby that will provide him with a lifetime of delightful leisure-time activity.

Some of the values of coins are less obvious than others. To collectors, every coin represents a slice of history—the date, design and legends on a coin tie it to a particular time and place and often to a famous person. The more a collector can tell about a coin, the more precious it becomes to him and to everyone with whom he shares his knowledge. Books such as *Hidden Values in Coins* provide this kind of valuable background information that can enrich your collecting experience.

6. MINTING METHODS

Coins have been issued for over two thousand years. In that time the methods of striking coins have gone through a transformation just as radical as the change from ox-cart to jet plane.

Ancient coins

It is generally agreed that the ancient Greeks were the first to make coins of a standard shape, a standard size, a standard content, and a standard value established by the state. Most of the coins were silver, of which the Greeks had an ample supply. Some were gold, and others were made of electrum (an alloy of gold and silver).

Up to comparatively modern times, coins were struck by a process that we would today consider very crude. When we use terms like "standard shape" and "standard size," we have to make allowances for the lack of precise coining equipment.

First, an artist or craftsman would prepare a design that was sunk into a thick bronze disk. (This is called an "intaglio" design.) When this die of the obverse, or face of the coin, was completed, it was placed snugly in a pit hollowed out of the top of an anvil.

The next step was to carve a second intaglio design on the bottom of a bronze punch. This design was intended for the reverse (or "tail" side of the coin). Meanwhile disks of silver of the desired size and weight were subjected to enough heat in a nearby furnace to make them soft enough to receive the impressions from the dies.

The minting process was a simple affair in ancient Greece. The disk was placed on the lower die (right). Then the upper die (left) was placed on top of it and struck with a hammer.

The minter picked up the disks with a tongs and one at a time placed them over the obverse die in the anvil. The man, with the bronze punch in his left hand, placed it on top of the obverse die. Then he hit the punch several times with a hammer. Thus, the bottom side of the disk took the impression of the obverse die, while the top side of the disk took the design of the reverse die from the punch. The man then removed the newly made coin with his tongs and left the coin to cool and harden. These ancient coins were not exactly round, nor uniformly thick and the details depended upon the minter's ability and the temperature of the metal.

A handsome coin of ancient times. Gela, about 485 B.C., silver tetradrachm, *reverse:* man-headed bull (river god).

(Left) Mantua, about 1500, silver testone, *obverse:* Francisco II Gonzaga; (right) *reverse:* melting pot in flames. A gem of Renaissance coinage.

121

This method, suitable for a simple national economy which needed very few coins, was used up to about the middle of the seventeenth century.

Renaissance coinage

About 1500 A.D. the volume of business began to expand considerably and precious metals began to stream in from the New World in considerable quantities. The improvement in mining techniques also helped to increase the supply of metal, and ingenious men began to think of devising more effective coining methods.

During the Renaissance, some of the most celebrated artists of the time designed coins and became interested in devising machinery for striking coins. Donato Bramante, one of the most famous architects in Italy, invented such machinery, and Leonardo da Vinci improved it. Gradually this equipment spread to other countries, but it took a long time before the new methods were fully accepted.

During the reign of Elizabeth I (1558-1603) in England, a Frenchman named Eloye Mestrelle, who came to live in England, introduced a milling machine which rolled metal to any desired thickness, cut out the blanks, and stamped the designs on them.

The new coins were superior in all respects to the old hand-hammered type. Another innovation that Mestrelle introduced was corrugating the edges of the coins — that is, putting vertical grains on them — to discourage anyone from clipping or shaving metal off the edges.

Since Mestrelle's machinery appeared at a time when the scientific and mechanical revolution was just getting under way, he had to use power sources that seem very rudimentary to our way of thinking. He had to rely on horse power or water pressure. Even so, his techniques were too advanced for his time. The staff of the Mint feared that his new-fangled methods would lead to wholesale dismissals. The result was a series of intrigues that led to Mestrelle's hanging in 1578 on the probably trumped-up charge of forgery.

(Left) England, 1653, silver crown, *obverse:* shield of St. George in wreath; (right) *reverse:* shield of St. George and Ireland in wreath. One of the most beautiful English coins made by the old hand-hammered method.

Mestrelle's sad fate naturally discouraged other inventors, and almost a century passed before mechanical production was adopted in England. This came about in 1662 during the reign of Charles II. To guard against clipping, the edges of many of the coins of this period have the legend *Decus et Tutamen* ("Decoration and Safeguard") inscribed on the edge.

The actual process of stamping coins was still very much like what it had been in ancient times. The screw-press pictured on the next page was only a more efficient version of the old hammer method.

The lower die was fastened into the base of the press. The upper die was fastened to the bottom of the screw shaft. A horizontal bar was used to turn the screw that lowered the shaft to make the impression. A workman grasped the handle at the right-hand end of the bar. After a coin blank was placed on the lower die, he revolved the bar until the shaft made contact with the blank. Further pressure then produced the obverse and reverse designs on the coin.

Once the coin was struck, the bar was flipped back, raising the shaft and making room for another coin blank. Continual repetition of this hand process turned out about twenty coins — or a little more — a minute. The earliest United States coins were struck in this way.

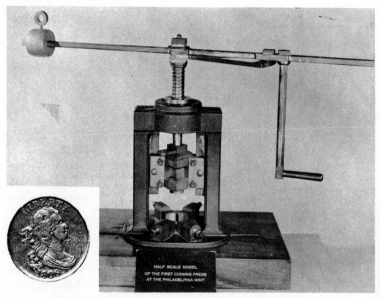

This early screw-press was worked by hand. The operator turned the handle at the right, forcing the die in the center to press down on the metal placed at the bottom of the press. (Inset) An early American coin struck on the screw press: a half cent (draped bust type) issued in 1806.

Beginning of modern coinage

After James Watt invented a workable and efficient steam engine, he and his partner, Matthew Boulton, soon realized that their new power machinery was ideally suited to speed up the production of coins. In 1790 they demonstrated that a single engine could power eight presses, turning out 50 large coins or 150 small coins per minute. Seven years later Watts and Boulton began working for the Mint in London. Their first coin was the famous "Cartwheel" twopenny.

Modern minting methods

Nowadays the making of coins has been mechanized to an uncanny degree of efficiency. To begin with, all coins of a given

(Left) England, 1797, copper twopenny, *obverse:* George III; (right) *reverse:* Britannia. The famous "Cartwheel," so called because of its weight and size.

type have a standardized content. For example, every penny contains 950 parts copper to 50 parts zinc. In the case of silver coins, 900 parts silver are alloyed with 100 parts copper. The metals are weighed in huge quantities on a remarkably sensitive balance that is accurate to one-hundredth of an ounce.

After weighing, the metals pass to an electric furnace, where they are melted. The alloy is prepared in a liquid state and formed into thin bars in molds. Two checking processes verify the proportions in the alloyed metal.

The bars are then passed through several rollers to be softened and stretched into thin strips. The bars used for pennies end up as strips eight feet long and 48/1000th of an inch thin.

An American coin struck in modern times: Half dollar, 1950, *reverse:* Liberty Bell.

Ingenious punch machines hammer 500 blank coins out of each strip, four at a time. The wasted metal is gathered and melted down for future use. When the punching process is over the blanks are too hard for immediate use, and they are softened by means of an annealing process. But this introduces a new complication, as it stains the blanks; so they are passed to machines which wash and dry them.

The blanks are now ready for the milling machine, which thickens the edges to make the coins last longer. At last they are ready to have designs stamped on them by automatic, high-speed machines in the Press Room. A pressure of 40 tons is enough for stamping pennies, whereas silver dollars (which have not been coined since 1935) required a pressure of 160 tons. Such a press produces 10,000 finished coins in a single hour.

Before the silver coins are weighed, their edges are corrugated. Corrugating the coins makes them more durable, and also serves as a protection against counterfeiting. Even the most skillful counterfeiter cannot match the corrugating techniques used in the Mint.

The finished coins now pass to automatic machines that weigh them, count them, and pack them — 5,000 ($50 value) to a bag. They are now ready to be put into circulation.

Detecting counterfeits

Counterfeiting of coins is much less frequent nowadays than it was formerly. The United States Secret Service stresses these four dependable ways of detecting counterfeit coins:

1. When dropped, genuine coins have a bell-like ring, whereas counterfeit coins have a dull sound.

2. Counterfeit coins are generally greasy to the touch.

3. Genuine coins have regular, even corrugations on their edges. Counterfeit coins will show irregularities in this respect.

4. It is often possible to cut counterfeit coins with a knife, whereas with genuine coins this is difficult or impossible.

Here is a vivid example of one of the outstanding differences between a genuine coin and a counterfeit coin. On the good coin the corrugated outer edge (known as the "reeding") is even and distinct. On the counterfeit coin, the ridges are crooked and indistinct.

7. CATALOG OF COINS

Half Cents

LIBERTY CAP TYPE

Year	Fair	Fine
1793	$125.00	$650.00
1794	$30.00	$150.00
1795 lettered edge, pole	$35.00	125.00
1795 lettered edge, 1,795	35.00	125.00
1795 plain edge, 1,795	30.00	125.00
1795 plain edge, no pole	30.00	125.00
1796 plain edge	400.00	2500.00
1797 lettered edge—rare	135.00	650.00
1797 plain edge	25.00	125.00
1797 1 over 1	20.00	100.00

TURBAN HEAD TYPE

Year	Very Good	Unc.
1809 normal date	$7.50	$50.00
1809 over 6	10.00	70.00
1810	12.50	175.00
1811	35.00	500.00
1825	7.50	75.00
1826	7.50	55.00
1828 12 stars	7.50	125.00
1828 13 stars	7.50	50.00
1829	7.50	45.00
1832	6.00	40.00
1833	6.00	40.00
1834	6.00	40.00
1835	6.00	40.00

DRAPED BUST TYPE

	Very Good	Fine
1800	$10.00	$17.50
1802 over 1800	100.00	175.00
1803	9.50	22.50
1804 plain 4, stems	30.00	40.00
1804 plain 4, no stems	9.00	15.00
1804 crosslet 4, stems	8.50	12.50
1804 crosslet 4, no stems	10.00	17.50
1804 spiked chin	10.00	15.00
1805 small 5, stems	85.00	135.00
1805 large 5, stems	10.00	15.00
1805 small 5, no stems	10.00	15.00
1806 small 6, stems	40.00	75.00
1806 small 6, no stems	10.00	15.00
1806 large 6, stems	10.00	15.00
1807	10.00	16.50
1808 over 7	45.00	100.00
1808	10.00	20.00

BRAIDED HAIR TYPE

	Very Good	
1849 large date	$8.50	$90.00
1850	7.50	75.00
1851	6.00	50.00
1853	6.00	55.00
1854	6.50	55.00
1855	6.50	55.00
1856	7.50	60.00
1857	12.50	75.00

Large Cents

Year	Good	Fine
1793 chain; Ameri	$250.00	$850.00
1793 chain; America	175.00	750.00
1793 chain; period after date	200.00	800.00
1793 wreath; vines and bars	$125.00	$450.00
1793 wreath; lettered edge	140.00	500.00
1793 Liberty Cap	275.00	1250.00
1794 (many varieties)	15.00	70.00
1795 lettered edge	25.00	90.00
1795 plain edge	12.50	65.00
1796 Liberty Cap	25.00	90.00

DRAPED BUST TYPE

Year	Very Good	Very Fine
1796 draped bust	$50.00	$135.00
1796 "Liherty"	60.00	175.00
1797 crudely milled	15.00	60.00
1797 plain edge ('96 rev.)	60.00	200.00
1797 stems on wreath	25.00	85.00
1797 no stems	40.00	125.00
1798 over 97	35.00	125.00
1798	15.00	50.00
1798 with 1796 reverse	40.00	135.00
1799 over 98	550.00	2000.00
1799	500.00	1850.00
1800 over 1798	17.50	50.00
1800 over 179	15.00	50.00
1800 perfect date	9.50	40.00
1801	15.00	50.00
1801 three-error variety	50.00	175.00
1801 1/000	22.50	85.00
1801 1/100 over 1/000	22.50	85.00
1802	7.50	30.00
1802 no stems	12.50	35.00
1802 1/000	17.50	65.00
1803 stems, small date	7.50	40.00
1803 no stems, small date	22.50	60.00
1803 1/100 over 1/000	22.50	75.00
1803 large date, fraction	85.00	225.00

Year	Very Good	Very Fine
1803 large date, small fraction	$135.00	$350.00
1804	275.00	750.00
1805 blunt 1	12.50	50.00
1806	30.00	100.00
1807 over 6	15.00	50.00
1807	12.50	45.00
1807 comet type	22.50	65.00

TURBAN HEAD TYPE

Year	Very Good	Very Fine
1808 13 stars	$17.50	$75.00
1808 12 stars	20.00	85.00
1809	90.00	325.00
1810 over 9	17.50	60.00
1810	15.00	55.00
1811 over 10	40.00	185.00
1811	35.00	175.00
1812	15.00	45.00
1813	30.00	100.00
1814	15.00	50.00

CORONET TYPE

Year	Very Good	Unc.
1816	$4.50	$90.00
1817 13 stars	3.00	75.00
1817 15 stars	6.50	175.00
1818	3.50	85.00
1819 over 18	5.00	150.00
1819	3.50	95.00
1820 over 19	4.50	90.00
1820	3.00	85.00
1821	15.00	300.00
1822	3.50	150.00
1823 over 22	20.00	1400.00
1823 normal date	20.00	1750.00
1824 over 22	10.00	350.00
1824	5.50	200.00
1825	4.50	140.00
1826 over 25	12.50	250.00
1826	4.50	150.00

LARGE CENTS — CORONET TYPE
(continued)

Year	Very Good	Unc.
1827	$3.50	$100.00
1828 large date	3.50	100.00
1828 small date	6.50	175.00
1829	3.50	85.00
1830 large letters	3.00	85.00
1830 small letters	12.50	200.00
1831	3.50	75.00
1832	4.00	125.00
1833	3.50	75.00
1834	4.00	85.00
1835 old head	4.00	85.00
1835 new head	3.75	75.00
1836	3.00	75.00
1837	2.50	85.00
1837 beaded hair	2.75	90.00
1838	2.50	60.00

BRAIDED HAIR TYPE

Year	Very Good	Unc.
1839 over 36	$110.00	$1250.00
1839 type as 38	6.50	125.00
1839 silly head	7.50	150.00
1839 booby head	5.50	125.00
1839 type as 1840	6.50	150.00
1840	4.50	85.00
1841	4.00	85.00
1842	3.75	90.00
1843 type as 1842	4.00	75.00
1843 obverse of 1842 and reverse of 1844	15.00	300.00
1843 type as 1844	5.00	110.00
1844	3.00	75.00
1845	3.00	55.00
1846 tall date	2.50	40.00
1846 small date	2.50	30.00
1847	2.50	55.00
1848	2.50	55.00
1849	2.50	55.00
1850	2.50	55.00
1851	2.50	50.00
1852	2.50	55.00
1853	2.50	50.00
1854	3.00	55.00

Year	Very Good	Unc.
1855	3.00	55.00
1856	3.00	55.00
1857	20.00	125.00

Flying Eagle Cents
(*White Copper-Nickel, thick*)

Year	Very Good	Unc.
1856 rare	$900.00	$3,000.00
1857	6.00	100.00
1858 large letters	7.50	140.00
1858 small letters	7.00	130.00

Indian Head Cents
(*White Copper-Nickel, thick*)

Year	Very Good	Unc.
1859	$ 5.00	$ 75.00
1860	4.50	55.00
1861	10.00	110.00
1862	4.00	30.00
1863	2.50	25.00
1864	6.50	60.00

(*Bronze*)

Year	Very Good	Unc.
1864	$4.50	$60.00
1864 L on ribbon rare	30.00	300.00
1865	3.00	45.00
1866	15.00	135.00
1867	15.00	135.00
1868	16.00	165.00
1869 over 68	60.00	650.00
1869	25.00	325.00
1870	20.00	165.00
1871	30.00	200.00
1872	40.00	275.00
1873	8.50	95.00
1874	7.50	95.00
1875	7.50	95.00
1876	11.50	110.00
1877	175.00	1000.00
1878	12.50	110.00
1879	3.00	40.00
1880	2.25	30.00
1881	2.25	26.00
1882	2.25	26.00
1883	1.75	25.00
1884	3.00	40.00
1885	6.50	60.00
1886	4.00	45.00
1887	1.25	22.50
1888	1.25	25.00

Year	Very Good	Unc.
1889	$ 1.25	$ 22.50
1890	1.25	20.00
1891	1.25	20.00
1892	1.50	24.00
1893	1.25	20.00
1894	3.50	45.00
1895	1.00	20.00
1896	1.00	27.50
1897	.90	22.50
1898	.90	20.00
1899	.90	20.00
1900	.75	12.50
1901	.65	10.00
1902	.65	10.00
1903	.65	10.00
1904	.65	11.50
1905	.65	10.00
1906	.65	10.00
1907	.65	10.00
1908	.75	15.00
1908 S	30.00	140.00
1909	1.50	15.00
1909 S	110.00	400.00

Lincoln Head Cents

Year	Very Good	Unc.
1909 VDB	$1.00	$6.50
1909 S VDB	150.00	350.00
1909 plain	.35	8.50
1909 S plain	32.50	115.00
1910	.30	10.00
1910 S	4.75	50.00
1911	.30	10.00
1911 S	11.50	75.00
1911 D	2.00	45.00
1912	.30	12.50
1912 S	7.50	60.00
1912 D	2.50	55.00
1913	.35	13.50
1913 S	5.00	55.00
1913 D	2.00	50.00
1914	.75	35.00
1914 S	6.00	100.00
1914 D	55.00	700.00
1915	1.85	100.00
1915 S	5.00	60.00
1915 D	1.25	25.00
1916	.30	9.50
1916 S	1.00	35.00
1916 D	.65	22.50
1917	.35	10.00
1917 S	.65	30.00
1917 D	.75	30.00

Year	Very Good	Unc.
1918	.25	10.50
1918 S	.75	37.50
1918 D	.75	37.50
1919	.20	9.00
1919 S	.50	20.00
1919 D	.50	22.50
1920	.20	9.00
1920 S	.75	45.00
1920 D	.75	45.00
1921	.65	20.00
1921 S	2.00	175.00
1922	60.00	600.00
1922 D	4.50	75.00
1923	.20	9.00
1923 S	2.25	240.00
1924	.20	17.50
1924 S	2.00	95.00
1924 D	17.50	165.00
1925	.20	9.00
1925 S	.75	40.00
1925 D	.40	30.00
1926	.20	7.50
1926 S	10.00	140.00
1926 D	.45	27.50
1927	.20	7.50
1927 S	1.00	50.00
1927 D	.40	25.00
1928	.20	7.00
1928 S	.65	32.50
1928 D	.40	20.00
1929	.15	5.00
1929 S	.20	6.00
1929 D	.20	10.00
1930	.15	3.50
1930 S	.30	7.50
1930 D	.25	10.00
1931	.65	30.00
1931 S	35.00	85.00
1931 D	6.00	85.00
1932	1.00	20.00
1932 D	.90	18.50
1933	1.00	22.50
1933 D	4.00	35.00

Quantity	Year	Unc.
219,080,000	1934	$3.50
28,446,000	1934 D	20.00
245,388,000	1935	1.65
38,702,000	1935 S	6.00
47,000,000	1935 D	4.00
309,637,569	1936	1.00
29,130,000	1936 S	3.50
40,620,000	1936 D	2.50
309,179,320	1937	1.25
34,500,000	1937 S	2.25
50,430,000	1937 D	1.75
156,696,734	1938	2.50
15,180,000	1938 S	6.50

LINCOLN HEAD CENTS (continued)

Quantity	Year	Unc.
20,010,000	1938 D	$ 4.00
316,479,520	1939	1.25
52,070,000	1939 S	2.25
15,160,000	1939 D	6.50
586,825,872	1940	1.00
112,940,000	1940 S	1.35
81,390,000	1940 D	1.65
887,039,100	1941	1.50
92,360,000	1941 S	2.75
128,700,000	1941 D	3.00
657,828,600	1942	.80
85,590,000	1942 S	5.00
206,698,000	1942 D	.65
684,628,670	1943 zinc-steel	.55
191,550,000	1943 S zinc-steel	2.00
217,660,000	1943 D zinc-steel	.90
1,435,400,000	1944 copper	.40
282,760,000	1944 S copper	.75
430,578,000	1944 D copper	.50
1,040,515,000	1945 copper	.55
181,770,000	1945 S copper	.65
226,268,000	1945 D copper	.60

Bronze (prewar composition)

Quantity	Year	Unc.
991,655,000	1946	.40
198,100,000	1946 S	.65
315,690,000	1946 D	.55
190,555,000	1947	1.00
99,000,000	1947 S	1.50
194,750,000	1947 D	.55
317,570,000	1948	.75
81,735,000	1948 S	1.75
172,637,500	1948 D	.60
217,490,000	1949	1.00
64,290,000	1949 S	2.50
154,370,500	1949 D	.90
272,686,386	1950	.75
118,505,000	1950 S	1.25
334,950,000	1950 D	.45
294,633,500	1951	.80
100,890,000	1951 S	1.50
625,355,000	1951 D	.40
186,856,980	1952	.75
137,800,004	1952 S	1.25
746,130,000	1952 D	.35
256,883,800	1953	.40
181,835,000	1953 S	1.00
700,515,000	1953 D	.30
71,873,350	1954	1.00
96,190,000	1954 S	.75
251,552,500	1954 D	.30
330,958,200	1955	.25
	1955 double strike	450.00
44,610,000	1955 S	1.75
563,257,500	1955 D	.25

Quantity	Year	Unc.
420,926,081	1956	$ .20
1,098,201,100	1956 D	.15
282,540,000	1957	.15
1,051,342,000	1957 D	.15
252,595,000	1958	.20
800,953,300	1958 D	.10
619,715,000	1959	.10
1,279,760,000	1959 D	.10
586,405,000	1960 small date	12.50
	1960 large date	.10
1,580,884,000	1960 D small date	.75
	1960 D large date	.10
756,373,244	1961	.10
1,753,266,700	1961 D	.10
609,263,019	1962	.10
1,793,148,400	1962 D	.10
757,185,645	1963	.10
1,774,020,400	1963 D	.10
	1964	.10
	1964 D	.10
	1965	.10

TWO CENTS — BRONZE

Year	Very Good	Unc.
1864 small motto	$35.00	$265.00
1864 large motto	1.50	27.50
1865	1.75	25.00
1866	2.50	30.00
1867	2.50	30.00
1868	2.50	30.00
1869	3.00	30.00
1870	4.00	42.50
1871	5.00	55.00
1872	35.00	100.00
1873 only proofs were struck		

Three Cents—Nickel

Year	Very Good	Unc.
1865	$ 1.50	$ 17.50
1866	1.75	17.50
1867	1.75	17.50
1868	1.75	17.50
1869	2.00	17.50
1870	2.00	20.00
1871	3.50	30.00
1872	3.00	27.50
1873	2.50	25.00
1874	3.50	30.00
1875	6.00	37.50
1876	6.00	37.50
1877 only proofs were struck		
1878 only proofs were struck		
1879	7.50	35.00
1880	7.50	35.00
1881	2.00	17.50
1882	6.00	35.00
1883	6.00	35.00
1884	6.50	42.50
1885	6.50	42.50
1886 only proofs were struck		
1887	17.50	100.00
1887 over 86—only proofs		
1888	4.50	30.00
1889	4.50	30.00

Three Cents—Silver

Year	Very Good	Unc.
1851	$ 4.50	$ 37.50
1851 O	10.00	100.00
1852	3.00	35.00
1853	3.00	35.00
1854	7.50	45.00
1855	12.50	120.00
1856	6.50	60.00
1857	6.00	60.00
1858	5.50	50.00
1859	6.00	50.00
1860	6.00	35.00
1861	5.50	35.00
1862	5.50	35.00
1863 (all remaining years		
1864 struck as proofs only)		
1865		
1866		
1867		
1868		
1869		
1870		
1871		
1872		
1873		

Nickel Five Cents

SHIELD TYPE

Year	Very Good	Unc.
1866	$ 7.50	$100.00
1867 with rays	10.00	150.00
1867 without rays	2.50	25.00
1868	2.50	25.00
1869	3.50	30.00
1870	5.00	32.50
1871	35.00	165.00
1872	5.00	35.00
1873	5.00	37.50
1874	7.50	38.00
1875	15.00	90.00
1876	7.50	40.00
1877 only proofs were struck		
1878 only proofs were struck		
1879	17.50	60.00
1880	20.00	65.00
1881	15.00	55.00
1882	2.75	22.50
1883	3.00	27.50

LIBERTY HEAD NICKELS

Year	Very Good	Unc.
1883 without "Cents"	$1.50	$7.50
1883 with "Cents"	5.50	37.50
1884	6.00	37.50
1885	65.00	250.00
1886	32.50	125.00
1887	3.75	35.00
1888	6.50	32.50
1889	3.50	30.00
1890	4.50	32.50
1891	3.50	30.00
1892	3.50	30.00
1893	3.50	30.00
1894	6.00	50.00
1895	2.50	35.00
1896	3.50	50.00
1897	1.75	25.00
1898	1.75	25.00
1899	1.50	22.50
1900	1.00	20.00
1901	.75	20.00
1902	.75	20.00
1903	.75	20.00
1904	.75	20.00
1905	.75	20.00
1906	.75	20.00
1907	.75	20.00
1908	.75	20.00
1909	1.00	22.50
1910	.75	18.50
1911	.75	18.50
1912	.75	18.50

LIBERTY HEAD NICKELS (continued)

Year	Very Good	Unc.
1912 D	3.00	200.00
1912 S	35.00	390.00
1913 (an outstanding rarity)		

BUFFALO NICKELS

Year	Very Good	Unc.
1913 Type 1—buffalo on mound	$1.65	$8.50
1913 S Type 1	6.50	37.50
1913 D Type 1	4.25	27.50
1913 Type 2—buffalo on plane	2.00	12.50
1913 S Type 2	35.00	125.00
1913 D Type 2	21.50	85.00
1914	1.75	20.00
1914 S	5.50	65.00
1914 D	19.00	95.00
1915	1.50	17.50
1915 S	8.50	125.00
1915 D	5.50	60.00
1916	.75	12.50
1916 S	3.50	65.00
1916 D	4.25	65.00
1917	.75	12.50
1917 S	5.00	125.00
1917 D	4.50	85.00
1918	1.25	40.00
1918 S	5.00	165.00
1918 D	4.50	160.00
1918 D over 7(rare)	215.00	5000.00
1919	.65	25.00
1919 S	6.00	200.00
1919 D	5.00	220.00
1920	.65	17.50
1920 S	3.50	175.00
1920 D	4.50	185.00
1921	1.25	45.00
1921 S	14.50	285.00
1923	.65	14.00
1923 S	4.00	165.00
1924	.65	17.50
1924 S	8.50	535.00
1924 D	4.50	145.00
1925	.65	17.50
1925 S	6.50	225.00
1925 D	7.50	175.00
1926	.65	15.00
1926 S	9.50	350.00
1926 D	4.00	350.00
1927	.45	15.00
1927 S	4.00	250.00
1927 D	1.75	40.00

Year	Very Good	Unc.
1928	.45	12.50
1928 S	1.00	45.00
1928 D	.65	12.50
1929	.35	9.00
1929 S	.50	13.50
1929 D	.50	12.50
1930	.35	12.50
1930 S	1.25	40.00
1931 S	4.75	65.00
1934	.30	10.00
1934 D	.50	15.00
1935	.25	4.50
1935 S	.35	7.50
1935 D	.35	10.00
1936	.30	3.75
1936 S	.40	4.50
1936 D	.40	4.00
1937	.25	4.50
1937 S	.70	5.00
1937 D	.60	4.25
1937 D three-legged buffalo	75.00	215.00
1938 D	.70	3.50

JEFFERSON NICKELS

Quantity	Year	Ext. Fine	Unc.
19,515,365	1938	$ .75	$4.00
4,105,000	1938 S	6.50	13.50
5,376,000	1938 D	4.00	11.50
120,627,535	1939	.60	2.50
6,630,000	1939 S	6.50	22.50
3,514,000	1939 D	25.00	65.00
176,499,158	1940	.50	1.25
39,690,000	1940 S	.75	2.75
43,540,000	1940 D	.50	2.00
203,283,720	1941	.35	1.00
43,445,000	1941 S	.65	2.50
53,432,000	1941 D	.50	2.25
49,818,600	1942	.45	3.00
13,938,000	1942 D	4.50	22.50

Wartime Silver Content

Quantity	Year		Unc.
57,900,600	1942 P		11.50
32,900,000	1942 S		6.00
271,165,000	1943 P		3.00
104,060,000	1943 S		2.75
15,294,000	1943 D		8.50
119,150,000	1944 P		3.50
21,640,000	1944 S		6.50
32,309,000	1944 D		2.75
119,408,100	1945 P		5.00
58,939,000	1945 S		2.50
37,158,000	1945 D		2.50

Prewar Nickel Content

Quantity	Year	Unc.
161,116,000	1946 ....$	.75
13,560,000	1946 S	2.75
45,292,200	1946 D	1.25
95,000,000	1947	.85
24,720,000	1947 S	2.50
37,822,000	1947 D	1.40
89,348,000	1948	.75
11,300,000	1948 S	3.50
44,734,000	1948 D	2.75
60,652,000	1949	1.60
9,716,000	1949 S	6.00
35,238,000	1949 D	2.25
9,847,386	1950	6.50
2,630,030	1950 D	27.50
26,689,500	1951	3.00
7,776,000	1951 S	9.50
20,460,000	1951 D	3.00
64,069,980	1952	1.00
20,572,000	1952 S	2.00
30,638,000	1952 D	5.75
46,772,800	1953	.85
19,210,900	1953 S	1.75
59,878,600	1953 D	.75
47,917,350	1954	.65
29,384,000	1954 S	1.00
117,183,060	1954 D	.50
8,266,200	1955	4.50
74,464,100	1955 D	.85
35,397,081	1956	.60
67,222,040	1956 D	.50
38,408,000	1957	.60
136,828,900	1957 D	.30
17,088,000	1958	1.25
168,249,120	1958 D	.25
27,248,000	1959	.60
160,738,240	1959 D	.25
55,416,000	1960	.30
192,582,180	1960 D	.20
76,668,244	1961	.20
229,372,760	1961 D	.15
100,602,019	1962	.15
280,195,720	1962 D	.15
178,851,645	1963	.15
276,829,460	1963 D	.15
	1964	.15
	1964 D	.15
	1965..............................	.15

Half Dimes

BUST TYPE

Year	Good	Very Fine
1794 ....$125.00		$500.00
1795	75.00	375.00
1796	100.00	400.00
1796 over 5	200.00	750.00
1797 13 stars..............	100.00	550.00
1797 15 stars..............	75.00	400.00
1797 16 stars..............	85.00	475.00
1800	75.00	325.00
1800 LIBEKTY	85.00	400.00
1801	75.00	450.00
1802 extremely rare ..1500.00		6000.00
1803	60.00	375.00
1805	125.00	600.00

Year	Very Good	Unc.
1829	$4.00	$55.00
1830	3.00	50.00
1831	3.00	45.00
1832	3.00	45.00
1833	3.00	45.00
1834	3.00	45.00
1835	3.00	45.00
1836	3.00	45.00
1837 large 5c	4.00	50.00
1837 small 5c	10.00	90.00

LIBERTY SEATED TYPE

1837 no stars $35.00		$250.00
1838 O no stars	45.00	450.00
1838 stars	3.00	45.00
1839	2.00	32.50
1839 O	4.50	42.50
1840	2.50	40.00
1840 O	5.00	75.00
1840 drapery	2.50	40.00
1840 O drapery	7.50	85.00
1841	2.00	35.00
1841 O	4.00	90.00
1842	2.00	20.00
1842 O	6.00	125.00
1843	2.00	30.00
1844	4.50	37.50
1844 O	8.50	100.00
1845	2.25	25.00
1846	45.00	250.00
1847	2.25	25.00
1848	2.50	27.50
1848 O	6.00	100.00

Year	Very Good	Unc.
1849	2.50	27.50
1849 over 48	4.00	50.00
1849 O	30.00	300.00
1850	2.00	30.00
1850 O	4.00	75.00
1851	2.00	25.00
1851 O	4.00	85.00
1852	2.00	25.00
1852 O	6.00	100.00
1853 no arrows	11.50	75.00
1853 arrows	2.00	35.00
1853 O no arrows	65.00	500.00
1853 O arrows	3.00	35.00
1854 arrows	2.00	25.00
1854 O arrows	2.50	35.00
1855 arrows	2.00	25.00
1855 O arrows	3.50	60.00
1856	1.25	25.00
1856 O	2.00	27.50
1857	1.50	25.00
1857 O	2.00	35.00
1858	1.50	25.00
1858 O	2.00	27.50
1859	3.00	35.00
1859 O	2.50	35.00
1860 no stars	1.75	25.00
1860	3.00	30.00
1861	2.00	25.00
1862	2.00	25.00
1863	12.50	85.00
1863 S	10.00	75.00
1864 (Struck in proof only)		
1864 S	12.50	100.00
1865	12.50	75.00
1865 S	7.50	75.00
1866	12.50	75.00
1866 S	10.00	75.00
1867	10.00	75.00
1867 S	6.00	60.00
1868	5.00	30.00
1868 S	3.00	30.00
1869	3.00	30.00
1869 S	3.00	35.00
1870	1.50	25.00
1871	1.50	25.00
1871 S	10.00	75.00
1872	1.50	25.00
1872 S in wreath	2.50	25.00
1872 S below wreath	3.00	25.00
1873	2.50	25.00
1873 S	3.50	30.00

Dimes

BUST TYPE

Year	Good	Very Fine
1796	$200.00	$925.00
1797 13 stars	150.00	750.00
1797 16 stars	165.00	750.00
1798 over 97	60.00	425.00
1798	50.00	400.00
1800	45.00	285.00
1801	65.00	400.00
1802	70.00	425.00
1803	60.00	410.00
1804	100.00	485.00
1805	40.00	215.00
1807	27.50	200.00
1809	30.00	150.00
1811 over 09	17.50	85.00
1814	7.50	40.00
1820	4.50	35.00
1821	4.00	20.00
1822	25.00	200.00
1823 over 22	6.00	45.00
1824 over 22	7.50	50.00
1825	5.00	27.50
1827	5.00	25.00
1828 large date	15.00	80.00
1828 small date	7.50	40.00

Year	Very Good	Unc.
1829 large 10c	$10.00	$100.00
1829 medium 10c	7.00	85.00
1829 small 10c	3.50	70.00
1830	3.00	60.00
1831	3.00	60.00
1832	3.00	60.00
1833	3.00	70.00
1834	3.00	60.00
1835	3.00	60.00
1836	3.00	60.00
1837	4.00	75.00

LIBERTY SEATED TYPE

Without stars

1837	$30.00	$250.00
1838 O	40.00	400.00

DIMES — LIBERTY SEATED TYPE
(continued)

With stars, no drapery from elbow

Year	Very Good	Unc.
1838	$4.50	$70.00
1839	3.00	45.00
1839 O	4.00	50.00
1840	3.00	40.00
1840 O	3.75	45.00
1841 very rare		

With drapery from elbow

1840	6.50	55.00
1841	2.00	35.00
1841 O	2.50	55.00
1842	2.00	35.00
1842 O	3.50	55.00
1843	2.00	35.00
1843 O	15.00	200.00
1844	25.00	250.00
1845	2.00	35.00
1845 O	7.00	80.00
1846	15.00	125.00
1847	4.00	50.00
1848	3.50	45.00
1849	2.00	30.00
1849 O	6.00	100.00
1850	2.00	25.00
1850 O	6.00	60.00
1851	1.75	25.00
1851 O	4.50	60.00
1852	1.50	25.00
1852 O	5.00	70.00
1853	15.00	125.00

With arrows at date

1853	$2.00	$35.00
1853 O	4.00	35.00
1854	1.50	27.50
1854 O	1.75	30.00
1855	1.75	27.50

Without arrows at date

1856	$1.75	$22.50
1856 O	2.50	37.50
1956 S	35.00	250.00
1857	1.75	25.00
1857 O	2.25	32.50
1858	1.50	30.00
1858 O	4.00	45.00
1858 S	20.00	225.00
1859	2.25	30.00
1859 O	2.25	45.00
1859 S	16.50	140.00
1860 S	12.50	100.00

Year	Very Good	Unc.
1860	$2.00	$20.00
1860 O rare	75.00	600.00
1861	1.50	20.00
1861 S	12.50	120.00
1862	2.00	20.00
1862 S	11.00	100.00
1863	12.50	60.00
1863 S	11.00	110.00
1864	10.00	50.00
1864 S	10.00	75.00
1865	10.00	55.00
1865 S	12.50	90.00
1866	12.50	60.00
1866 S	10.00	100.00
1867	12.50	60.00
1867 S	10.00	85.00
1868	2.00	20.00
1868 S	6.50	60.00
1869	2.00	22.50
1869 S	6.00	50.00
1870	2.00	20.00
1870 S	45.00	250.00
1871	2.00	20.00
1871 S	11.00	110.00
1871 CC rare	175.00	1250.00
1872	1.75	20.00
1872 S	12.50	75.00
1872 CC	100.00	750.00
1873 no arrows	1.75	22.50
1873 arrows	9.00	85.00
1873 S arrows	12.50	100.00
1873 CC arrows	300.00	1500.00
1873 CC no arrows(unique)		
1874 arrows	8.50	90.00
1874 S arrows	15.00	145.00
1874 CC arrows (very rare)	100.00	850.00

Without arrows at date

1875	$1.25	$20.00
1875 S in wreath	1.75	20.00
1875 S below wreath	1.75	17.50
1875 CC in wreath	1.75	20.00
1875 CC below wreath	3.50	35.00
1876	1.25	15.00
1876 S	1.75	25.00
1876 CC	2.00	25.00
1877	1.00	20.00
1877 S	1.75	22.50

DIMES — LIBERTY SEATED TYPE
(continued)

Year	Very Good	Unc.
1877 CC	$1.75	$22.50
1878	1.25	20.00
1878 CC	12.50	75.00
1879	9.00	40.00
1880	9.00	35.00
1881	10.00	35.00
1882	1.00	20.00
1883	1.00	20.00
1884	1.00	20.00
1884 S	7.50	65.00
1885	1.00	20.00
1885 S	65.00	400.00
1886	1.00	20.00
1886 S	8.50	55.00
1887	1.00	20.00
1887 S	2.00	27.50
1888	1.00	20.00
1888 S	2.00	25.00
1889	1.00	20.00
1889 S	7.50	115.00
1890	1.00	20.00
1890 S	1.75	27.50
1891	1.00	20.00
1891 O	2.00	35.00
1891 S	1.50	27.50

LIBERTY HEAD TYPE

Year	Very Good	Unc.
1892	$1.25	$17.50
1892 O	2.75	30.00
1892 S	20.00	95.00
1893	2.50	17.50
1893 O	6.00	55.00
1893 S	6.00	50.00
1894	4.00	25.00
1804 O	42.50	275.00
1894 S ext. rare		13,500.00
1895	30.00	150.00
1895 O	65.00	675.00
1895 S	10.00	100.00
1896	3.75	25.00
1896 O	27.50	185.00
1896 S	35.00	235.00
1897	1.25	15.00
1897 O	30.00	200.00
1897 S	9.50	100.00
1898	1.00	15.00
1898 O	6.00	115.00
1898 S	5.00	80.00
1899	1.00	15.00
1899 O	5.00	100.00
1899 S	4.50	65.00
1900	1.25	15.00
1900 O	5.00	90.00
1900 S	3.25	50.00

Year	Very Good	Unc.
1901	$ .75	$15.00
1901 O	3.00	85.00
1901 S	45.00	500.00
1902	.65	13.50
1902 O	2.50	60.00
1902 S	5.00	75.00
1903	.65	13.50
1903 O	2.00	45.00
1903 S	15.00	140.00
1904	.75	15.00
1904 S	12.50	100.00
1905	.75	15.00
1905 O	2.50	65.00
1905 S	1.75	30.00
1906	.75	15.00
1906 D	1.25	17.50
1906 O	3.00	30.00
1906 S	2.00	25.00
1907	.60	15.00
1907 D	1.50	32.50
1907 O	1.75	27.50
1907 S	1.75	27.50
1908	.65	12.50
1908 D	.75	15.00
1908 O	3.00	37.50
1908 S	2.25	25.00
1909	.60	15.00
1909 D	4.00	47.50
1909 O	4.50	50.00
1909 S	4.00	50.00
1910	.60	50.00
1910 D	1.00	25.00
1910 S	2.50	35.00
1911	.60	15.00
1911 D	.75	17.50
1911 S	1.75	25.00
1912	.60	15.00
1912 D	.85	17.50
1912 S	2.00	37.50
1913	.60	15.00
1913 S	12.50	165.00
1914	.60	15.00
1914 D	.85	17.50
1914 S	1.75	35.00
1915	.75	15.00
1915 S	2.50	30.00
1916	.60	15.00
1916 S	.75	20.00

MERCURY HEAD TYPE

Year	Very Good	Unc.
1916	$ .60	$7.50
1916 D rare	135.00	750.00
1916 S	1.00	15.00
1917	.50	7.50
1917 D	1.50	60.00
1917 S	.85	22.50

DIMES — MERCURY HEAD TYPE
(continued)

Year	Very Good	Unc.
1918	.45	25.00
1918 D	1.25	40.00
1918 S	1.00	27.50
1919	.40	27.50
1919 D	2.50	100.00
1919 S	2.25	130.00
1920	.50	12.50
1920 D	.85	35.00
1920 S	.85	35.00
1921	15.00	300.00
1921 D	20.00	250.00
1923	.50	12.50
1923 S	1.50	82.50
1924	.45	15.00
1924 D	1.35	75.00
1924 S	1.50	67.50
1925	.45	15.00
1925 D	3.00	300.00
1925 S	1.00	90.00
1926	.45	12.50
1926 D	1.00	50.00
1926 S	5.50	300.00
1927	.45	9.00
1927 D	1.50	200.00
1927 S	1.00	100.00
1928	.45	11.50
1928 D	1.00	95.00
1928 S	.85	55.00
1929	.30	6.75
1929 D	.60	15.00
1929 S	.75	18.50
1930	.45	15.00
1930 S	2.00	40.00
1931	1.25	20.00
1931 D	5.00	65.00
1931 S	3.00	50.00
1934	.25	7.50
1934 D	.50	15.00
1935	.25	4.00
1935 D	.50	25.00
1935 S	.40	8.50

Quantity	Year	Unc.
87,504,130	1936	$2.75
16,132,000	1936 D	17.50
9,210,000	1936 S	9.50
56,865,756	1937	3.00
14,146,000	1937 D	6.00
9,740,000	1937 S	7.50
22,198,728	1938	3.00
5,537,000	1938 D	8.50
8,090,000	1938 S	6.50
67,749,321	1939	2.00
24,394,000	1939 D	2.50
10,540,000	1939 S	6.50

Quantity	Year	Unc.
65,361,827	1940	$2.00
21,198,000	1940 D	2.00
21,560,000	1940 S	2.25
175,106,557	1941	1.50
45,634,000	1941 D	2.75
43,090,000	1941 S	3.00
205,432,329	1942 over 1 (F 100.00; VF125.00, EF175.00)	400.00
	1942	1.50
60,740,000	1942 D	1.50
49,300,000	1942 S	3.00
191,710,000	1943	1.50
71,949,000	1943 D	1.50
60,400,000	1943 S	1.50
231,410,000	1944	1.50
62,224,000	1944 D	1.50
49,490,000	1944 S	1.50
159,130,000	1945	1.50
40,245,000	1945 D	1.50
41,920,000	1945 S	1.50

DIMES — ROOSEVELT TYPE

Quantity	Year	Unc.
255,250,000	1946	$ .75
61,043,500	1946 D	1.60
27,900,000	1946 S	2.50
121,520,000	1947	2.00
46,835,000	1947 D	1.65
38,840,000	1947 S	2.25
74,950,000	1948	4.00
52,841,000	1948 D	2.00
35,520,000	1948 S	2.25
30,940,000	1949	11.50
26,034,000	1949 D	4.00
13,510,000	1949 S	17.50
50,181,500	1950	2.50
46,803,000	1950 D	2.00
20,440,000	1950 S	15.00
103,937,602	1951	2.00
52,191,800	1951 D	1.75
31,630,000	1951 S	15.00
99,122,073	1952	1.00
122,100,000	1952 D	.90
44,419,500	1952 S	6.50
53,618,920	1953	1.50
136,400,000	1953 D	.75
39,180,000	1953 S	1.50
114,243,503	1954	.50
106,397,000	1954 D	.45
22,860,000	1954 S	1.50

DIMES — ROOSEVELT TYPE
(continued)

Quantity	Year	Unc.
12,828,381	1955	$3.25
13,959,000	1955 D	2.75
18,510,000	1955 S	1.75
108,821,081	1956	.45
108,015,100	1956 D	.40
160,160,000	1957	.40
113,354,330	1957 D	.35
31,910,000	1958	1.25
136,564,600	1958 D	.40
85,780,000	1959	.45
164,919,790	1959 D	.35
70,390,000	1960	.40
200,160,400	1960 D	.30
96,758,244	1961	.40
209,146,550	1961 D	.25
75,668,019	1962	.30
334,948,380	1962 D	.25
126,725,645	1963	.25
421,476,530	1963 D	.25
	1964	.20
	1964 D	.20
	1965	.20

Quarters

BUST TYPE

Year	Good	Very Fine
1796 rare	$600.00	$2500.00
1804	125.00	650.00
1805	60.00	250.00
1806 over 5	50.00	250.00
1806	40.00	200.00
1807	40.00	250.00
1815	17.50	135.00
1818 over 15	18.50	140.00
1818	15.00	75.00
1819	17.50	75.00
1820	17.50	70.00
1821	17.50	70.00
1822	18.50	100.00
1822 25 over 50c (rare)	150.00	550.00
1823 over 22 (extremely rare)	600.00	2250.00
1824	25.00	100.00
1825 over 22	17.50	65.00
1825 over 23	17.50	65.00
1825 over 24	17.50	65.00
1827 extremely rare		
1828	15.00	65.00
1828 25 over 50c	50.00	175.00

Year	Very Good	Unc.
1831	$10.00	$115.00
1832	10.00	100.00
1833	12.50	125.00
1834	10.00	100.00
1835	7.50	90.00
1836	10.00	100.00
1837	10.00	100.00
1838	9.00	100.00

Twenty Cents

Year	Very Good	Unc.
1875	$22.50	$125.00
1875 S	17.50	100.00
1875 CC	25.00	150.00
1876	25.00	150.00
1876 CC (extremely rare)		7,500.00
1877 only proofs were struck		
1878 only proofs were struck		

LIBERTY SEATED TYPE

Without drapery from elbow

1838	$10.00	$85.00
1839	7.50	75.00
1840 O	7.50	75.00

With drapery from elbow

1840	7.50	75.00
1840 O	7.50	70.00
1841	15.00	100.00
1841 O	6.00	60.00

QUARTERS — LIBERTY SEATED TYPE
(continued)

Year	Very Good	Unc.
1842	7.00	60.00
1842 O large date	7.50	60.00
1842 O small date	15.00	100.00
1843	5.00	40.00
1843 O	5.00	50.00
1844	5.00	50.00
1844 O	5.00	50.00
1845	5.00	40.00
1846	5.00	40.00
1847	5.00	37.50
1847 O	6.00	40.00
1848	6.00	50.00
1849	5.00	40.00
1849 O	85.00	500.00
1850	6.00	50.00
1850 O	5.00	50.00
1851	5.00	50.00
1851 O	6.00	85.00
1852	5.50	60.00
1852 O	12.50	75.00
1853 over 52	60.00	400.00

With arrows at date. Rays over eagle.

Year	Very Good	Unc.
1853	5.00	65.00
1853 O	8.50	75.00

With arrows at date. Without rays.

Year	Very Good	Unc.
1854	4.00	45.00
1854 O	5.00	50.00
1855	4.00	50.00
1855 O	50.00	400.00
1855 S	50.00	385.00

Without arrows at date

Year	Very Good	Unc.
1856	3.50	20.00
1856 O	4.00	25.00
1856 S	25.00	225.00
1857	3.00	20.00
1857 O	3.50	25.00
1857 S	25.00	250.00
1858	3.50	20.00
1858 O	4.50	35.00
1858 S	27.50	235.00
1859	3.75	20.00
1859 O	5.50	25.00
1859 S	27.50	235.00
1860	3.50	25.00
1860 O	5.00	27.50
1860 S	20.00	250.00
1861	3.25	25.00
1861 S	18.50	200.00
1862	3.50	25.00
1862 S	15.00	175.00
1863	5.00	30.00

Year	Very Good	Unc.
1864	5.00	35.00
1864 S	17.50	225.00
1865	6.00	35.00
1865 S	12.50	175.00

With motto over eagle

Year	Very Good	Unc.
1866	6.00	40.00
1866 S	17.50	175.00
1867	5.50	40.00
1867 S	17.50	150.00
1868	6.50	40.00
1868 S	12.50	125.00
1869	6.00	45.00
1869 S	12.50	120.00
1870	4.00	35.00
1870 CC	135.00	850.00
1871	4.50	30.00
1871 S	12.50	125.00
1871 CC	125.00	650.00
1872	4.00	30.00
1872 S	20.00	120.00
1872 CC	185.00	1250.00
1873 no arrows	7.50	50.00
1873 CC no arrows	500.00	2500.00

With arrows at date

Year	Very Good	Unc.
1873	20.00	150.00
1873 S	27.50	165.00
1873 CC	400.00	1750.00
1874	22.50	150.00
1874 S	27.50	165.00

Without arrows at date

Year	Very Good	Unc.
1875	3.00	20.00
1875 S	8.50	95.00
1875 CC	10.00	110.00
1876	3.00	20.00
1876 S	3.00	20.00
1876 CC	3.50	30.00
1877	3.00	17.50
1877 S	3.00	22.50
1877 CC	3.50	35.00
1878	3.00	20.00
1878 S	150.00	850.00
1878 CC	6.00	50.00
1879	16.50	50.00
1880	16.50	50.00
1881	16.50	50.00
1882	15.00	50.00
1883	15.00	50.00
1884	20.00	60.00
1885	16.50	50.00
1886	27.50	100.00
1887	17.50	75.00
1888	17.50	75.00
1888 S	3.50	25.00

QUARTERS — LIBERTY SEATED TYPE
(continued)

Year	Very Good	Unc.
1889	$17.50	$45.00
1890	6.00	27.50
1891	3.00	20.00
1891 O	85.00	475.00
1891 S	3.50	27.50

LIBERTY HEAD (BARBER) TYPE

Year	Very Good	Unc.
1892	$1.50	$27.50
1892 O	4.50	45.00
1892 S	15.00	150.00
1893	1.25	25.00
1893 O	3.50	50.00
1893 S	4.50	60.00
1894	1.75	27.50
1894 O	4.50	65.00
1894 S	3.25	60.00
1895	1.50	25.00
1895 O	3.50	115.00
1895 S	5.00	75.00
1896	1.65	25.00
1896 O	7.50	250.00
1896 S	150.00	1350.00
1897	1.50	25.00
1897 O	10.00	145.00
1897 S	11.50	175.00
1898	1.25	25.00
1898 O	3.75	100.00
1898 S	4.00	100.00
1899	1.25	25.00
1899 O	3.50	85.00
1899 S	8.50	100.00
1900	1.00	25.00
1900 O	4.00	85.00
1900 S	3.25	100.00
1901	1.00	17.50
1901 O	17.50	365.00
1901 S	325.00	2000.00
1902	1.00	25.00
1902 O	4.00	75.00
1902 S	6.00	110.00
1903	1.00	25.00
1903 O	4.50	175.00
1903 S	7.50	175.00
1904	1.00	25.00
1904 O	8.50	290.00
1905	1.00	25.00
1905 O	7.50	175.00
1905 S	6.00	80.00
1906	1.00	25.00
1906 D	2.50	30.00
1906 O	3.00	45.00
1907	1.00	25.00
1907 D	2.50	32.50
1907 O	1.50	27.50

Year	Very Good	Unc.
1907 S	$3.00	$70.00
1908	1.00	25.00
1908 D	1.25	27.50
1908 O	1.25	27.50
1908 S	6.50	90.00
1909	1.00	25.00
1909 D	1.35	27.50
1909 O	18.50	350.00
1909 S	3.50	62.50
1910	1.50	30.00
1910 D	2.25	32.50
1911	1.00	25.00
1911 D	3.00	57.50
1911 S	3.50	60.00
1912	1.00	25.00
1912 S	4.50	120.00
1913	6.00	90.00
1913 D	2.50	42.50
1913 S	160.00	1500.00
1914	1.00	25.00
1914 D	1.15	25.00
1914 S	12.50	325.00
1915	1.15	26.50
1915 D	1.00	25.00
1915 S	2.75	47.50
1916	1.25	32.50
1916 D	1.25	26.00

STANDING LIBERTY TYPE

Year	Very Good	Unc.
1916	$400.00	$1200.00
1917 type I*	4.00	32.50
1917 D type I*	7.50	45.00
1917 S type I*	7.50	55.00
1917 type II**	4.00	27.50
1917 D type II**	8.50	65.00
1917 S type II**	8.50	65.00
1918	4.50	50.00
1918 D	6.50	75.00
1918 S	4.50	50.00
1918 S over 17	275.00	2750.00
1919	5.00	50.00
1919 D	30.00	250.00
1919 S	32.50	300.00
1920	3.00	25.00
1920 D	13.50	135.00
1920 S	6.50	70.00
1921	22.50	200.00
1923	3.00	20.00
1923 S	45.00	250.00
1924	3.00	25.00
1924 D	6.50	45.00
1924 S	8.50	80.00
1925	1.00	20.00
1926	1.00	20.00

* stars at sides of eagle
** 3 stars below eagle

QUARTERS — STANDING LIBERTY TYPE
(continued)

Year	Very Good	Unc.
1926 D	$1.50	$25.00
1926 S	3.50	125.00
1927	1.00	20.00
1927 D	2.50	70.00
1927 S	7.50	550.00
1928	1.00	20.00
1928 D	1.50	22.50
1928 S	1.00	20.00
1929	.75	17.50
1929 D	1.25	35.00
1929 S	1.25	22.50
1930	.75	17.50
1930 S	1.25	25.00

WASHINGTON TYPE

Year	Fine	Unc.
1932	$1.25	$15.00
1932 D	35.00	250.00
1932 S	32.50	110.00
1934	1.00	15.00
1934 D	2.50	60.00
1935	1.00	8.50
1935 D	1.75	50.00
1935 S	2.00	40.00
1936	1.00	7.50
1936 D	8.50	250.00
1936 S	2.00	30.00
1937	1.00	7.50
1937 D	1.15	12.50
1937 S	5.00	65.00
1938	3.50	50.00
1938 S	2.50	30.00
1939	1.00	8.50
1939 D	1.00	10.00
1939 S	2.00	30.00
1940	1.00	10.00
1940 D	3.00	40.00
1940 S	1.00	7.00

Quantity	Year	Unc.
79,047,287	1941	$3.00
16,714,800	1941 D	5.00
16,080,000	1941 S	6.50
102,117,123	1942	3.50
17,487,200	1942 D	3.00
19,384,000	1942 S	22.50
99,700,000	1943	1.75
16,095,600	1943 D	3.50
21,700,000	1943 S	7.00
104,956,000	1944	1.75
14,600,000	1944 D	2.50
12,560,000	1944 S	3.00

Quantity	Year	Unc.
74,372,000	1945	$1.50
12,341,600	1945 D	2.50
17,004,001	1945 S	2.25
53,436,000	1946	1.40
9,072,800	1946 D	3.50
4,204,000	1946 S	5.50
22,556,000	1947	1.75
15,338,400	1947 D	2.00
5,532,000	1947 S	5.50
35,196,000	1948	1.25
16,766,800	1948 D	1.75
15,960,000	1948 S	2.00
9,312,000	1949	15.00
10,068,400	1949 D	4.00
24,971,512	1950	2.50
21,075,600	1950 D	1.50
10,284,600	1950 S	4.50
43,505,602	1951	1.25
35,354,800	1951 D	1.25
8,948,000	1951 S	7.50
38,862,073	1952	1.25
49,795,200	1952 D	1.00
13,707,800	1952 S	3.50
18,664,920	1953	3.50
56,112,400	1953 D	.85
14,016,000	1953 S	1.50
54,645,503	1954	.75
46,305,000	1954 D	1.25
11,834,722	1954 S	1.50
18,558,381	1955	1.75
3,182,400	1955 D	4.50
44,325,081	1956	.65
32,334,500	1956 D	.75
46,720,000	1957	.60
77,924,160	1957 D	.50
6,360,000	1958	2.00
78,124,900	1958 D	.50
24,384,000	1959	.60
62,054,232	1959 D	.50
29,164,000	1960	.55
63,000,324	1960 D	.50
40,064,244	1961	.50
83,656,928	1961 D	.50
39,374,019	1962	.50
127,554,756	1962 D	.50
77,391,645	1963	.50
135,288,184	1963 D	.50
	1964	.50
	1964 D	.50
	1965	.50

Half Dollars

BUST TYPE

Year	Very Good	Very Fine
1794	$250.00	$975.00
1795	150.00	525.00
1796 15 stars	$1500.00	$4250.00
1796 16 stars	2000.00	4250.00
1797	1750.00	3750.00
1801	100.00	350.00
1802	100.00	300.00
1803	50.00	150.00
1805 over 4	65.00	180.00
1805	30.00	95.00
1806 over 5	42.50	125.00
1806 over 9 (inverted 6)	75.00	250.00
1806	30.00	85.00
1807 bust right	30.00	85.00

Year	Fine	Unc.
1807 bust left	$27.50	$200.00
1807 50 over 20	30.00	215.00
1808 over 7	25.00	100.00
1808	15.00	75.00
1809	13.50	75.00
1810	13.50	75.00
1811	12.00	60.00
1811 as 18.11	22.50	110.00
1812 over 11	22.50	140.00
1812	12.50	70.00
1813	12.50	70.00
1814 over 13	25.00	130.00
1814	13.50	65.00
1815 over 12	145.00	600.00
1817 over 13	30.00	130.00
1817	12.50	60.00
1817 as 181.7	35.00	125.00
1818	11.50	45.00
1818 over 17	12.50	60.00
1819 over 18	11.00	55.00
1819	9.50	47.50
1820 over 19	17.50	75.00
1820	17.50	75.00
1821	10.00	37.50
1822	10.00	37.50
1822 over 21	75.00	250.00
1823 over 22	35.00	85.00
1823	10.00	35.00
1824 over other dates	11.50	47.50
1824 over 21	11.50	45.00
1824	10.00	30.00

Year	Fine	Unc.
1825	$10.00	$30.00
1826	10.00	30.00
1827 over 26	22.50	95.00
1827	8.00	27.50
1828	10.00	32.50
1829 over 21	12.00	45.00
1829	9.00	30.00
1830	8.50	28.50
1831	8.50	28.50
1832	8.50	28.50
1833	8.50	25.00
1834	8.50	25.00
1835	7.50	25.00
1836 lettered edge	7.50	25.00
1836 milled edge	80.00	250.00
1837	30.00	95.00
1838	25.00	85.00
1838 O (extremely rare)		7500.00
1839	18.50	85.00
1839 O mint mark on obv.	110.00	330.00

LIBERTY SEATED TYPE

Year	Very Good	Unc.
1839 no drapery	$30.00	$220.00
1839 with drapery	10.00	50.00
1840 small, letters	6.50	50.00
1840 large letters	30.00	200.00
1840 O	6.50	50.00
1841	8.00	65.00
1841 O	6.50	50.00
1842	4.50	40.00
1842 O small date	60.00	275.00
1842 O large date	4.50	45.00
1843	4.50	45.00
1843 O	4.50	45.00
1844	4.50	45.00
1844 O	4.50	45.00
1845	5.50	55.00
1845 O	5.00	45.00
1846 error horizontal 6	45.00	225.00
1846	5.00	40.00
1846 O small date	5.00	40.00
1846 O large date	30.00	190.00
1847 over 46	150.00	800.00
1847	5.00	45.00
1847 O	5.00	45.00

HALF DOLLARS — LIBERTY SEATED TYPE
(continued)

Year	Very Good	Unc.
1848	$5.00	$45.00
1848 O	4.50	42.50
1849	4.50	42.50
1849 O	4.50	42.50
1850	30.00	135.00
1850 O	6.50	45.00
1851	10.00	125.00
1851 O	5.00	40.00
1852	30.00	240.00
1852 O	22.50	145.00
1853 O no arrows (extremely rare)		
1853 arrows	7.50	90.00
1853 O arrows	7.50	95.00
1854	5.00	45.00
1854 O	5.00	45.00
1855	6.00	65.00
1855 O	4.50	45.00
1855 S	45.00	425.00
1856	4.00	30.00
1856 O	4.00	30.00
1856 S	15.00	165.00
1857	3.50	30.00
1857 O	5.00	40.00
1857 S	20.00	200.00
1858	3.50	27.50
1858 O	4.00	25.00
1858 S	12.50	140.00
1859	4.00	27.50
1859 O	4.00	27.50
1859 S	10.00	85.00
1860	4.00	30.00
1860 O	4.00	27.50
1860 S	7.00	70.00
1861	4.00	27.50
1861 O	4.00	35.00
1861 S	5.00	50.00
1862	4.00	35.00
1862 S	4.50	45.00
1863	4.50	35.00
1863 S	4.50	40.00
1864	4.50	35.00
1864 S	4.50	40.00
1865	4.50	35.00
1865 S	4.50	40.00
1866 motto	6.00	40.00
1866 S no motto	55.00	350.00
1866 S motto..............	6.00	50.00
1867	5.00	45.00
1867 S	4.00	45.00
1868	5.00	45.00
1868 S	5.00	47.50
1869	5.00	35.00
1869 S	4.50	35.00
1870	4.50	32.50
1870 S	6.00	60.00

Year	Very Good	Unc.
1870 CC	$65.00	$575.00
1871	4.50	30.00
1871 S	5.00	45.00
1871 CC	50.00	450.00
1872	4.50	30.00
1872 S	6.00	55.00
1872 CC	45.00	300.00
1873 no arrows..........	4.50	35.00
1873 arrows	17.50	150.00
1873 CC no arrows....	50.00	350.00
1873 CC arrows	30.00	250.00
1873 S	25.00	190.00
1874	20.00	165.00
1874 S	30.00	225.00
1874 CC	50.00	450.00
1875	4.00	27.50
1875 S	4.00	27.50
1875 CC	6.50	75.00
1876	4.00	27.50
1876 S	4.00	27.50
1876 CC	6.50	45.00
1877	4.00	25.00
1877 S	4.00	30.00
1877 CC	6.00	45.00
1878	4.00	30.00
1878 S	350.00	3000.00
1878 CC	100.00	600.00
1879	45.00	80.00
1880	40.00	75.00
1881	40.00	75.00
1882	45.00	80.00
1883	37.50	75.00
1884	37.50	75.00
1885	37.50	75.00
1886	67.50	100.00
1887	37.50	90.00
1888	37.50	70.00
1889	37.50	70.00
1890	40.00	75.00
1891	7.50	50.00

LIBERTY HEAD (BARBER) TYPE

Year	Very Good	Unc.
1892	$3.50	$60.00
1892 O	27.50	120.00
1892 S	30.00	175.00
1893	3.00	60.00
1893 O	8.50	90.00
1893 S	27.50	135.00
1894	3.50	55.00
1894 O	6.00	120.00
1894 S	6.50	120.00
1895	3.00	60.00
1895 O	5.50	110.00
1895 S	8.50	120.00

HALF DOLLARS — LIBERTY HEAD
(BARBER) TYPE (continued)

Year	Very Good	Unc.
1896	$5.00	$60.00
1896 O	10.00	225.00
1896 S	30.00	325.00
1897	3.00	60.00
1897 O	30.00	325.00
1897 S	30.00	325.00
1898	2.50	60.00
1898 O	5.50	125.00
1898 S	5.00	120.00
1899	2.25	60.00
1899 O	4.25	120.00
1899 S	5.00	120.00
1900	2.25	60.00
1900 O	3.00	120.00
1900 S	3.00	115.00
1901	2.25	60.00
1901 O	8.50	365.00
1901 S	20.00	800.00
1902	2.50	60.00
1902 O	3.50	110.00
1902 S	4.50	225.00
1903	2.25	60.00
1903 O	3.50	180.00
1903 S	4.50	450.00
1904	2.00	60.00
1904 O	4.25	145.00
1904 S	17.50	425.00
1905	4.00	67.50
1905 O	7.50	185.00
1905 S	3.00	100.00
1906	1.75	60.00
1906 D	2.25	62.50
1906 O	2.75	70.00
1906 S	3.75	105.00
1907	1.75	60.00
1907 D	2.25	62.50
1907 O	2.50	65.00
1907 S	3.75	135.00
1908	1.75	60.00
1908 D	1.75	62.50
1908 O	2.00	62.50
1908 S	3.50	95.00
1909	1.50	65.00
1909 O	3.50	100.00
1909 S	3.00	90.00
1910	3.50	75.00
1910 S	3.00	85.00
1911	1.75	60.00
1911 D	3.00	75.00
1911 S	3.50	77.50
1912	1.75	60.00
1912 D	2.00	65.00
1912 S	2.75	75.00
1913	17.50	150.00

Year	Very Good	Unc.
1913 D	$3.00	$70.00
1913 S	4.50	165.00
1914	22.50	225.00
1914 S	3.50	95.00
1915	22.50	235.00
1915 D	2.00	65.00
1915 S	2.50	92.50

STANDING LIBERTY TYPE

Year	Very Good	Unc.
1916	$7.50	$85.00
1916 D on obverse	7.50	57.50
1916 S on obverse	20.00	135.00
1917	1.50	20.00
1917 D on obverse	7.50	90.00
1917 D on reverse	4.00	115.00
1917 S on obverse	12.50	450.00
1917 S on reverse	3.00	85.00
1918	1.75	90.00
1918 D	2.50	125.00
1918 S	2.00	100.00
1919	5.00	200.00
1919 D	7.50	400.00
1919 S	8.00	550.00
1920	1.75	45.00
1920 D	3.50	325.00
1920 S	3.00	300.00
1921	35.00	450.00
1921 D	45.00	650.00
1921 S	13.50	550.00
1923 S	2.00	225.00
1927 S	2.00	100.00
1928 S	2.00	100.00
1929 D	3.00	65.00
1929 S	2.00	65.00
1933 S	2.00	70.00
1934	.75	9.00
1934 D	.75	25.00
1934 S	1.00	55.00
1935	.75	9.00
1935 D	1.00	40.00
1935 S	1.75	50.00
1936	.75	8.50
1936 D	.75	15.00
1936 S	.85	35.00
1937	.75	12.50
1937 D	.85	40.00
1937 S	.85	40.00
1938	.75	17.50
1938 D	18.50	135.00
1939	.75	12.50
1939 D	.75	12.50
1939 S	.75	22.50

HALF DOLLARS
STANDING LIBERTY TYPE (continued)

Quantity	Year	Unc.
9,167,279	1940	$7.50
4,550,000	1940 S	13.50
24,207,412	1941	8.50
11,248,400	1941 D	12.50
8,098,000	1941 S	25.00
47,839,120	1942	5.00
10,973,800	1942 D	12.50
12,708,000	1942 S	15.00
53,190,000	1943	5.50
11,346,000	1943 D	9.00
13,450,000	1943 S	13.50
28,206,000	1944	5.50
9,769,000	1944 D	6.50
8,904,000	1944 S	9.00
31,502,000	1945	6.50
9,966,800	1945 D	6.50
10,156,000	1945 S	7.50
12,118,000	1946	7.00
2,151,100	1946 D	12.50
3,724,000	1946 S	9.50
4,094,000	1947	8.50
3,900,000	1947 D	8.50

Quantity	Year	Unc.
7,715,602	1960	$2.00
18,215,812	1960 D	1.50
11,318,244	1961	1.75
20,276,442	1961 D	1.50
12,932,019	1962	1.50
35,473,281	1962 D	1.50
25,239,645	1963	1.50
67,069,292	1963 D	1.25

KENNEDY TYPE

	Year	Unc.
	1964	$ .75
	1964 D	.75
	1965	.75

FRANKLIN TYPE

Quantity	Year	Unc.
3,006,814	1948	$11.50
4,028,600	1948 D	7.00
5,714,000	1949	45.00
4,120,600	1949 D	13.50
3,744,000	1949 S	27.50
7,793,509	1950	20.00
8,031,600	1950 D	13.50
16,859,602	1951	10.00
9,475,200	1951 D	11.50
13,696,000	1951 S	10.00
21,274,073	1952	5.00
25,395,600	1952 D	3.75
5,526,000	1952 S	10.00
2,796,920	1953	15.00
20,900,400	1953 D	2.50
4,148,000	1953 S	6.00
13,421,503	1954	2.75
25,445,580	1954 D	2.50
4,993,400	1954 S	4.25
2,876,381	1955	14.00
4,701,384	1956	4.50
6,361,952	1957	2.75
19,966,850	1957 D	2.00
4,917,652	1958	4.00
23,962,412	1958 D	1.75
7,349,291	1959	2.25
13,053,750	1959 D	1.75

Silver Dollars

BUST TYPE

Year	Very Good	Very Fine
1794 very rare	$1400.00	$4,500.00
1795	125.00	300.00
1795 new bust	100.00	275.00
1796	65.00	200.00
1797 stars 10 and 6	100.00	275.00
1797 stars 9 and 7	100.00	275.00
1798 small eagle, 15 stars	125.00	300.00
1798 small eagle, 13 stars	100.00	275.00
1798 large eagle	45.00	150.00
1799 over 98, 15 stars	65.00	200.00
1799 over 98, 13 stars	50.00	175.00
1799 stars 7 and 6	50.00	175.00
1799 stars 8 and 5	60.00	200.00
1800	65.00	160.00
1801	70.00	175.00
1802 over 1	65.00	160.00
1802	60.00	150.00
1803	60.00	150.00
1804 outstanding rarity	Unc.	36,000.00
1836 pattern, proof condition		1500.00
1838 pattern, proof condition		3500.00
1839 pattern, proof condition		3250.00

LIBERTY SEATED TYPE

Year	Very Good	Unc.	Year	Very Good	Unc.
1840	$15.00	$125.00	1859	15.00	110.00
1841	12.50	90.00	1859 O	10.00	75.00
1842	7.50	85.00	1859 S	22.50	175.00
1843	7.50	75.00	1860	15.00	90.00
1844	17.50	120.00	1860 O	10.00	75.00
1845	17.50	120.00	1861	15.00	115.00
1846	7.50	75.00	1862	22.50	150.00
1846 O	15.00	125.00	1863	17.50	150.00
1847	8.50	75.00	1864	12.50	135.00
1848	30.00	150.00	1865	12.50	125.00
1849	8.50	85.00	1866 motto	12.50	90.00
1850	35.00	250.00	1867	12.50	75.00
1850 O	20.00	100.00	1868	10.00	75.00
1851	300.00	1250.00	1869	10.00	70.00
1852	350.00	1750.00	1870	10.00	65.00
1853	25.00	200.00	1870 S extremely rare	Unc.	12,500.00
1854	40.00	250.00	1870 CC	30.00	350.00
1855	40.00	225.00	1871	6.50	60.00
1856	27.50	200.00	1871 CC	350.00	2000.00
1857	27.50	200.00	1872	6.50	60.00
1858 Struck in proof only, 1600.00					

DOLLARS — LIBERTY SEATED TYPE
(continued)

Year	Very Good	Unc.
1872 S	$35.00	$275.00
1872 CC	150.00	1250.00
1873	8.50	75.00
1873 CC	400.00	2250.00
1873 S extremely rare		

LIBERTY HEAD (MORGAN) TYPE

Year	Very Fine	Unc.
1878 8 feathers	$6.50	$17.50
1878 7 feathers	1.50	3.75
1878 7 over 8 feathers	10.00	25.00
1878 S	1.25	2.50
1878 CC	4.50	12.50
1879	1.25	2.50
1879 O	2.00	9.50
1879 S	1.50	3.50
1879 CC	10.00	175.00
1880	1.50	3.00
1880 O	1.50	5.00
1880 S	1.50	3.50
1880 CC	22.50	60.00
1881	1.50	4.50
1881 O	1.50	4.50
1881 S	1.50	3.00
1881 CC	35.00	65.00
1882	1.50	3.00
1882 O	1.50	4.50
1882 S	1.50	3.50
1882 CC	12.50	27.50
1883	1.25	2.75
1883 O	1.50	3.00
1883 S	2.00	25.00
1883 CC	10.00	27.50
1884	1.50	3.50
1884 O	1.50	3.00
1884 S	3.50	30.00
1884 CC	25.00	50.00
1885	1.50	2.50
1885 O	1.50	3.00
1885 S	4.50	22.50
1885 CC	40.00	65.00
1886	1.50	2.25
1886 O	3.50	25.00
1886 S	16.50	40.00
1887	1.50	3.50
1887 O	2.75	8.50
1887 S	9.00	25.00
1888	1.50	3.00
1888 O	1.50	4.50
1888 S	30.00	50.00
1889	1.25	2.50
1889 O	1.75	8.50
1889 S	30.00	60.00

Year	Fine	Unc.
1889 CC	$95.00	$675.00
1890	1.75	5.50
1890 O	1.50	5.00
1890 S	4.00	12.50
1890 CC	5.00	25.00
1891	4.00	17.50
1891 O	2.00	7.00
1891 S	6.50	22.50
1891 CC	11.00	27.50
1892	5.00	25.00
1892 O	3.50	16.00
1892 S	10.00	500.00
1892 CC	12.50	60.00
1893	13.50	75.00
1893 O	17.50	175.00
1893 S	300.00	4500.00
1893 CC	20.00	175.00
1894	75.00	300.00
1894 O	3.50	25.00
1894 S	10.00	50.00
1895 rare		
1895 O	12.50	160.00
1895 S	32.50	475.00
1896	1.50	4.00
1896 O	2.50	20.00
1896 S	12.50	165.00
1897	1.50	10.00
1897 O	3.50	15.00
1897 S	3.50	15.00
1898	1.50	5.00
1898 O	1.75	6.00
1898 S	3.50	35.00
1899	12.50	40.00
1899 O	1.25	2.25
1899 S	5.50	50.00
1900	1.25	3.00
1900 O	1.25	2.50
1900 S	3.50	25.00
1901	3.50	30.00
1901 O	1.25	2.50
1901 S	3.00	35.00
1902	2.00	7.50
1902 O	1.25	2.50
1902 S	14.00	50.00
1903	2.25	10.00
1903 O	25.00	45.00
1903 S	7.50	200.00
1904	3.00	18.50
1904 O	2.00	4.00
1904 S	3.50	165.00
1921	1.50	2.00
1921 S	1.50	7.50
1921 D	1.50	6.50

DOLLARS — PEACE TYPE

Quantity	Year	Ext. Fine	Unc.
1,006,473	1921	$20.00	$45.00
51,737,000	1922	2.00	3.00
15,063,000	1922 D	2.50	10.00
17,475,000	1922 S	2.50	10.00
30,800,000	1923	2.00	3.00
6,811,000	1923 D	4.00	17.50
19,020,000	1923 S	3.00	9.50
11,811,000	1924	2.00	5.00
1,728,000	1924 S	12.50	50.00
10,198,000	1925	2.00	5.00
1,610,000	1925 S	8.50	35.00
1,939,000	1926	10.00	25.00
2,348,700	1926 D	7.50	22.50
6,980,000	1926 S	4.00	15.00
848,000	1927	20.00	42.50
1,268,900	1927 D	15.00	40.00
866,000	1927 S	17.50	60.00
360,649	1928	75.00	150.00
1,632,000	1928 S	11.00	37.50
954,057	1934	20.00	40.00
1,569,000	1934 D	17.50	40.00
1,011,000	1934 S	60.00	325.00
1,576,000	1935	15.00	35.00
1,964,000	1935 S	10.00	45.00

TRADE DOLLARS

Quantity	Year	Very Good	Unc.
397,500	1873	$10.00	$100.00
703,000	1873 S	17.50	150.00
124,500	1873 CC	17.50	135.00
987,800	1874	7.50	35.00
2,549,000	1874 S	7.50	35.00
1,373,200	1874 CC	17.50	100.00
218,900	1875	12.50	75.00
4,487,000	1875 S	6.50	30.00
1,573,700	1875 CC	12.50	75.00
456,150	1876	7.50	35.00
5,227,000	1876 S	6.00	30.00
509,000	1876 CC	12.50	100.00
3,039,710	1877	6.00	37.50
9,519,000	1877 S	6.00	30.00
534,000	1877 CC	22.50	150.00
900	1878 Proofs only (very rare)		
4,162,000	1878 S	6.00	30.00
97,000	1878 CC	75.00	350.00
1,541	1879 Proofs only		
1,987	1880 Proofs only		
960	1881 Proofs only		
1,097	1882 Proofs only		
979	1883 Proofs only		
10	1884 Proofs only (rare)		
5	1885 Proofs only (very rare)		

PROOF SETS

Year	
1936	$1000.00
1937	400.00
1938	225.00
1939	200.00
1940	135.00
1941	120.00
1942	140.00
1950	160.00
1951	100.00
1952	60.00
1953	45.00
1954	30.00
1955	40.00
1956	17.50
1957	10.00
1958	20.00
1959	11.00
1960 large date	8.50
1960 small date	45.00
1961	7.00
1962	7.00
1963	8.00
1964	16.50

* includes both types of nickels issued in 1942

PRICE LIST OF FOREIGN COINS
ILLUSTRATED IN THIS VOLUME

LIST OF CONTROLLER COINS

LINCOLN HEAD CENTS: 1909S(VDB); 1909S; 1910S; 1911S; 1912S; 1913S; 1914D; 1914S; 1915S; 1921S; 1922D; 1923S; 1924D; 1924S; 1926S; 1931D; 1931S; 1933D. Other dates to watch are 1932; 1933; 1939D; 1954; 1955S; 1960 (small .date).

JEFFERSON NICKELS: 1938D; 1938S; 1939D; 1939S; 1942D. Other dates to watch are 1949S; 1950; 1950D; 1951S; 1955.

ROOSEVELT DIMES: 1949S; 1950S; 1951S; 1952S. Other dates to watch are 1947S; 1954S; 1955P; 1955D; 1955S.

WASHINGTON QUARTERS: 1932D; 1932S; 1936D; 1940D; 1955.

FRANKLIN HALF DOLLARS: 1948; 1949; 1953; 1955; 1956.

INDIAN HEAD CENTS: 1864 (L on ribbon); 1869; 1870; 1871: 1872; 1877; 1908S; 1909S.

BUFFALO HEAD NICKELS: D and S coins through 1928; 1937D (3-legged buffalo).

MERCURY HEAD DIMES: 1916D; 1919D; 1919S; 1921P; 1921D; 1926S; 1927D; 1942D (over '41). Other dates to watch are 1930S; 1931D; 1931S.

STANDING LIBERTY QUARTERS: 1916; 1917D, S (two varieties); 1918S (over '17); 1919D, S; 1923S; 1926S; 1927S. Other dates to watch are 1926D; 1927D; 1929D, S; 1930S.

STANDING LIBERTY HALF DOLLARS: 1916; 1917D, S; 1919P, D, S; 1921P, D, S; 1938D.

GLOSSARY

ALLOY: A combination of gold or silver or copper with one or more other metals. The purpose is to produce a coin of more durable and cheaper composition.

BULLION: Uncoined metal.

COMMEMORATIVE COIN: A coin issued to honor an outstanding event or individual.

CONDITION: The physical state of a coin — an important factor in determining its value.

CONTROLLER COINS: The comparatively rare — and hence the most valuable — coins of a given series.

CORRUGATED EDGE: Same as *Reeded Edge*.

COUNTERMARK: A stamp punched on a coin to indicate a new value or issuing authority.

DIE: A metal stamp used to impress the design on coins.

FACE VALUE: The denomination of a coin.

INSCRIPTION: Everything on the coin aside from pictorial elements. This would include any lettering and numbers.

INCUSE COIN: A coin on which the lettering and other details are sunk below the surface of the coin.

MARKET VALUE: The price at which a collector can buy a coin.

MILLED EDGE: A coin rim which has been raised in relation to the surface of the coin.

MINT MARK: A tiny letter struck on a coin to indicate the mint of origin.

NUMISMATICS: The science of coins and medals.

OBVERSE: The "head" of the coin — generally the side with the main design and date.

OVERSTRIKE: The striking of new material or design on an already existing coin, hiding all or some of the original coin.

PATTERN: A trial piece which may or may not be issued for general use.

PLANCHET: The blank from which a coin is struck.

PREMIUM VALUE: The price at which one can sell a coin (if above face value).

PROOF: A coin with a mirror-like surface struck with polished dies on a polished blank. Usually sold at a premium by the mints. Matte proofs (with a dull frosted surface) were struck by the United States during 1909-1916.

REEDED EDGE: A coin edge on which lines run across the thickness of the edge from obverse to reverse.

REVERSE: The "tail" of the coin — generally the side reserved for technical details, such as the denomination and mint mark.

ROLLS: A standard quantity of identical coins, all of the same type, same date, same mint.

TALER: A large silver coin first issued in various German states in the sixteenth century and later introduced into other countries. This term often appears in its English form ("dollar").

TYPE-COLLECTING: Collecting coins on the basis of the design. Example: Indian Head Cent, Lincoln Head Cent.

UP-GRADING: A continuous process of improving a collection by replacing inferior specimens with superior examples of the same coins.

VALUE: See *Face Value; Market Value; Premium Value.*

COIN FINDER

In identifying foreign coins, you will find it helpful to consult this list of inscriptions found on the most common foreign coins:

Belges, Belgie, Belgique	Belgium
Britt, Britan, Britannia, Britanniarum	Great Britain
Buenos Ayres	Argentina
Ceskoslovenska	Czechoslovakia
Danske	Denmark
Deutsches Reich	Germany
Eesti	Estonia
Eire	Ireland
Espanas	Spain
Fid Def Ind Imp	Great Britain
Filler	Hungary
Forint	Hungary
Francaise	France
Helvetia	Switzerland
Hispania	Spain
Island	Iceland
Kroner	Denmark, Norway
Kronor	Sweden
Magyar	Hungary
Markaa	Finland
Nederlanden	Netherlands
Oesterreich	Austria
Polska, Polski	Poland
Sede Vacante	Papal States
Suid Afrika	South Africa
Zloti, Zlotych	Poland

INDEX